OUIJA

THE MOST DANGEROUS GAME

OUIJA

THE MOST DANGEROUS GAME

STOKER HUNT

PERENNIAL LIBRARY

Harper & Row, Publishers
New York, Cambridge, Philadelphia, San Francisco
London, Mexico City, São Paulo, Singapore, Sydney

Grateful acknowledgment is made for permission to reprint an excerpt from *The Satan Trap* edited by Martin Ebon. Copyright © 1976 by Lomvard Associates, Inc. Reprinted by permission of Doubleday & Company, Inc.

FIRST EDITION

Designer: Abigail Sturges

Library of Congress Cataloging in Publication Data

Hunt, Stoker.
    Ouija, the most dangerous game.

    Includes index.
    1. Ouija board—Controversial literature.   I. Title.
BF1343.H86   1985   133.9'3   84-48166
ISBN   0-06-464095-7 (pbk.)

87   88   10   9   8   7   6   5   4

CONTENTS

ACKNOWLEDGMENTS

In addition to those mentioned in this book, the author wishes to thank the following people for their help and/ or encouragement: Boyce Batey, The Academy of Religion and Psychical Research; Bev Beltaire, P. R. Associates, Detroit; Larry Bernstein; Susan Blackmore, The Society for Psychical Research, London, England; Peter E. Blau, *The Baker Street Journal;* Peter Brewster, *The Toronto Sun;* Dennis Brown; Elsie Carper, *The Washington Post;* Lenny Cavallaro; Derek Coke-Kerr, Francis, Williams & Johnson, Edmonton, Alberta; Christine Cole; Robert Coly, Parapsychology Foundation, New York; Peter Courtney; Byron Dobell, *American Heritage;* John Douglas, CBC Radio, Toronto; Dick Fabian, *P. M. Magazine;* Dr. Tom Fagan, National Association of School Psychologists; Valdora Fike; Jim and Mary Fives; Kendrick Frazier, *The Skeptical Inquirer;* Lynn Gladhill, WLW Radio, Cincinnati; Bobbi and Joni Herrera; Dianne Hudson, *Late Night America,* PBS TV, Detroit; Gloria James; Laura F. Knipe, American Society for Psychical Research, New York; Tom Kneitel, *Popular Communications;* Tom Lafferty; Rudolf Marek; Robert Martin, *The Bay Area Review;* Brenda Marshall, The College of Psychic Studies, London, England; Pauline Mason, *The Toronto Sun;* Ken Meyer, WBZ Radio, Boston; John Miller; Nicki McWhirter, *The Detroit Free Press;* Philip Nyhius;

Eleanor O'Keeffe, The Society for Psychical Research, London, England; Tom Parteka; Ernie Piotrowski; Joseph Pivanko; Al Pollard, ESP Research Associates Foundation; Dan Proudfoot, *The Toronto Sun;* Andy Rapp, WUCM TV, Midland; Bonnie Reese; Michael Roberts, *The Midland Daily News;* Robert Ross; Esther Schupbach; Eileen Stein, *The Baltimore News American;* Joan Stoeker; Richard Strong, The Psychic Science Special Interest Group; Thelma Varney; Clement G. Vitek, *The Baltimore Sun;* Dolores Walker; Hal Youngblood, WJR Radio, Detroit; Nyla Young, The Coleman Library.

Special thanks go to Daniel Bial of Barnes & Noble and Irv Levey, Director of Barnes & Noble Books.

INTRODUCTION

Ouija experimenters sit tense above the board. Motionless they stare and wait. "Is someone here?" they whisper. "Will you talk with us this evening?"
Finally, something happens.
The pointer moves.

It answers—coherently, deliberately. And if you are one of those hunched over that board when it speaks, like it or not, you're experiencing a new dimension.

But what is happening? What force sends the planchette from letter to letter? Are you moving the pointer? Is your partner playing an elaborate joke on you? Impossible. Something is at work here. Something very unusual.

When you ask the board questions, it answers—*without* your deliberate influence. Whatever is happening, you are a part of it. You set out to explore the unusual, the paranormal, and now the unusual, the paranormal, seems to be exploring you!

The Ouija board can be incredibly exciting. It is both condemned and exalted. There are many who are violently against it and as many who are enthusiastically for it.

Ouija: The Most Dangerous Game takes a long, considered look at the talking board and some other devices and phenomena related to it—automatic writing, prophecy, dowsing, table-rapping, telepathy, obsession and possession.

Ouija invites controversy and provokes debate. Interpretive views at times overlap, but the basic debate is contradictory. It's a good example of one man's meat being another man's poison. There are those who insist that the board cripples and kills; others claim that it cures and creates. Many say it merely entertains. Who's telling the truth? Perhaps everybody.

In this book, I attempt to present all the interpretative views, pro and con, cool and hot, angelic and demonic. It is, I hope, an honest collection of conflicting ideas, fairly presented.

OUIJA
THE BASICS

1

THE HISTORY OF OUIJA

No one knows for certain where the name "Ouija"* originated. The *Encyclopedia of Occultism and Parapsychology* gives the following definition and history.

From the French *oui* and the German *ja*-yes. A wooden tripod on rollers which under the hand of the medium, moves over a polished board and spells out messages by pointing out letters with its apex. As an invention it is very old. It was used in the days of Pythagoras, about 540 B.C. According to a French historian's account of the philosopher's life, his sect held frequent seances or circles at which "a mystic table moving on wheels, moved towards signes which the philosopher and his pupil, Philolaus, interpreted to the audience as being revelations supposedly from the unseen world."

An improvement of the original Ouija board is the finger-like pointer at the narrow end and a simplification in the replacement of the wooden board by a piece of alphabetical cardboard. If the pointer and the roll at the apex is replaced by a

---

* Ouija is a registered trademark of Parker Brothers and is therefore capitalized throughout this book.

3

pencil thrust through a bored hole so as to form
the third leg, the Ouija board is transformed into
a planchette.

The nature of the Ouija phenomenon is controversial; so too
are its roots. No one person or culture can take credit for
its development. Ouija origins are multiple and ancient,
having been independently reinvented and rediscovered in a
wide variety of locations.

The Ouija is genuinely ancient in its origins. It is the
invention or discovery of many. In short, Ouija is nothing
less than a folk knowledge, a universal folk instrument.

• In China, centuries before the birth of Confucius (551?–
479 B.C.), the use of Ouija-like instruments was commonplace,
considered a nonthreatening way to communicate with the
spirits of the dead.

• In Greece, the philosopher and mathematician Pythagoras (ca 550 B.C.) encouraged his disciples to make use of
Ouija-like instruments to unearth revelations "from the
unseen world."

• In Rome, such instruments were popular as early as
the third century. A.D. In one famous case, three experimenters predicted the name of the person who would
succeed the reigning emperor. The three were tried for
treason, and Theodosius, the soldier named as successor by
the board, was executed.

• In thirteenth-century Tartary, the Mongols used Ouija-
like instruments for purposes of divination and instruction.

• In North America, long before Columbus' arrival, native
Indians used instruments they called squdilatc boards to
locate lost articles and missing persons. The board—which
had symbols instead of alphabet letters on it—also trans-
mitted information as to when and how certain religious
ceremonies should be performed.

• In France, a spiritualist named M. Planchette invented
an instrument in 1853 similar to the one Parker Brothers

now manufactures. This instrument had a small heart-shaped platform that rested on three legs, one of which was a pencil. When the planchette moved, the pencil wrote coherent messages. The use of this instrument became a fad throughout France and her empire.

Ouija in America— the Recent Developments

It's generally thought that the American inventor of the Ouija board was William Fuld in 1892; however, a year earlier a U.S. patent was issued to Elijah J. Bond as inventor of the Ouija board. According to a story that appeared in *American Heritage* magazine (April 1983), Fuld bought the rights from Bond in 1892 and filed for another patent. Fuld then founded The Southern Novelty Company in Baltimore, Maryland—later to be known as the Baltimore Talking Board Company—and began producing "Oriole Talking Boards."

William Fuld made a fortune from the board, but he was not an addicted Ouija user. "I'm no spiritualist!" he said. "I'm a Presbyterian. I built this factory on [the] Ouija's advice, but I haven't consulted the board since. Things have been moving along so well I didn't want to start anything."

The popularity of the talking board soared during World War I, when thousands of stay-at-home citizens turned to the Ouija in an attempt to keep in touch with sons, husbands and lovers who were fighting in Europe.

What appears to be a characteristic curve has developed in the board's sales history. Ouija sales peak during times of national catastrophe. So, bad times are good times for the makers of Ouija boards, and the thirties, forties and sixties witnessed national Ouija crazes.

At the University of Michigan, as reported by the New York *Tribune,* Dec. 24, 1919, the "Mysterious Talking Oracle" had "succeeded the Bible and the prayerbook in fraternity houses and students' rooms." The *New York Times Magazine* assaulted the Ouija by describing it as "the Bolshevik of the psychic realm." At one point the Baltimore *Sun* hired a full-time editor whose sole duty was to answer Ouija-related questions.

In 1966, Parker Brothers, one of the world's most successful producers of children's games, purchased the rights to the Ouija board and moved the operation from Baltimore to Salem, Massachusetts. The first full year after their takeover, Parker Brothers sold more than two million Ouija boards . . . topping the sales of their perennially best-selling board game, Monopoly.

Ouija Goes to Court

One of the questions this book must raise is whether the Ouija board is simply a game that is properly sold in toy shops and department stores alongside such children's favorites as Candyland, Sorry and Old Maid—or whether it is a more serious instrument, with the potential for hurting people. As far as the courts are concerned, the issue was settled more than sixty years ago.

In 1920, the Internal Revenue Service contended that the Ouija board was a game, and as such, taxable.

Arguing for the Baltimore Talking Board Company, Allen Fisher said, "We contend . . . that it [the Ouija board] is a form of amateur mediumship and not a game or sport. By means of this board one is enabled to get in touch with the other side." An attorney, Washington Bowie, supported this view when he described the board as "a medium of communication between this world and the next."

The court ruled against the Baltimore Talking Board Company—they would have to pay taxes. Circuit judge Knapp wrote a dissenting opinion. He said the Ouija board "is unique, in a class by itself, plainly different and distinguishable from any of the enumerated games!" But the majority opinion concluded:

It seems safe to say psychologists recognize the Ouija board as a real means of expression of automatism. The court knows in a general way that the Ouija board is seriously used by some persons in the belief that it affords mysterious spirit communication; by others as action by the subconscious or unconscious mind. But the court cannot pretend to be ignorant that it is very largely sold with the expectation that it is to be used merely as a means of social amusement or play, and is actually so used. It is true that automatism is the basis of this use, but phenomena of psychical nature may be the basis of amusement and games.

The Baltimore Talking Board Company petitioned the Supreme Court to hear the case, but the justices refused and the lower court ruling stood.

It certainly seems ironic that the Baltimore Talking Board Company maintained the Ouija board is not a game—though the success of the board was due to its availability in toy shops and game departments; and that the government took the position that Ouija was a game—though perhaps it should have been more interested in the dangers of unregulated psychic instruments.

In the mid-seventies an officer of the Craft, Game and Toy Group, an organization whose corporate membership then included Parker Brothers, said, "We know the game is made of ordinary components, manufactured by people not endowed with extraordinary powers. Our view is that the device is neutral, and that whatever power may be expressed through it comes from the players."

Is the Ouija board a game or is it not? As you will see, theologians, philosophers, educators, researchers, psychics and parapsychologists can't arrive at a common definition of the nature of the board. I'm certain that you'll come to your own conclusion by the time you've finished this book.

2

HOW THE BOARD WORKS

The question about the Ouija board being a game or not is controversial. Even more controversial is the question, How does the Ouija board work? Where do the messages actually come from?

There are two major theories. The spiritualist theory holds that the messages come from without; the automatistic (or "scientific") theory holds that the messages come from within. Arguments can be made for both theories.

The spiritualist theory is the older. It maintains that the spirits of dead souls use the Ouija board to communicate—and occasionally interact—with the living. Later in this book spiritualist experts will present the theories on who these spirits are, why they want to communicate with the living or why they need to interact with the living, their potential for good or for evil, what the spirits have to say, what they report from the world beyond, and the literary quality of their statements. We will also hear from noted religious leaders, for they too have many important and relevant things to say about the spiritualist theory.

The other major theory maintains that the working of the Ouija board—along with several other psychological and psychic phenomena—is an automatism. The dictionary defines automatism as "an action performed without the doer's intention or awareness." In other words, while the Ouija operator's conscious mind denies controlling the planchette, it is really the operator's *subconscious* mind controlling the muscles in the hand and arm, spelling out messages it needs or wants the conscious mind to hear.

The famous nineteenth-century scientist Michael Faraday was the first to perform an experiment that suggested how a psychic phenomenon—table-rapping—commonly considered spirit-induced, was actually an automatism. Very little research into the Ouija as automatism has been performed. But with the advent of Freudian theories of the unconscious, it somehow came to be accepted by a large group of people that the Ouija board was just another case of the subconscious trying to get messages to the conscious—the same way it does through dreams, or through other automatistic means such as psychosomatic illnesses or sleep-walking.

Later in this book we will hear about a psychiatrist who claimed that automatisms gained quicker insights into her patients' psyches than did hypnosis or other forms of traditional therapy. Also, Barbara Honegger, a well-known parapsychologist, offers an alternative theory on the mental processes going on during automatistic phenomena.

According to the responses we received in our 1983 national Ouija board survey, more than 30 percent of the respondents use the board to communicate with the dead. Almost as many try to get in touch with living people. The rest attempt to reach nonhuman "intelligences" (spirits, angels, pets, etc.) or try to find lost objects or attempt to develop their own psychic abilities. And some people go to the Ouija board for guidance. "Should I change jobs or ask for a raise?" "When is the best time to marry?" "What's this week's winning lottery number?" A communication with the dead might be for the purpose of locating a will or a family treasure.

Ouija Messages

The messages that come from or through the Ouija board most often take the form of a conversation. When people sit down at the Ouija board, ordinarily one of their first questions is, "Does anyone want to speak with us?" or "Are there any messages for us?" If there is no answer, the Ouija session will end. If contact is made—as usually happens—the "Other" will usually identify itself. It may be the spirit of a relative, friend or recently deceased celebrity. Given time, it may change names, personalities, or it may give way to another spirit who wants to communicate.

The "Other" often identifies itself as the spirit of a famous person. Religious, philosophical and political spirit voices are the most common, particularly Jesus, Saint John, Socrates, and Lincoln. The archangel Michael seems to be very popular as well.

There is no such thing as the typical Ouija message. As you will read in this book, the range of what people have experienced with the Ouija board is incredible. Your experience—if you choose to work with the board—will be entirely unpredictable.

The Form of the Messages

Spiritualist believers do not attempt to explain why Ouija messages seem to come from spirits. They *know* that they come from spirits, they say.

Non-spiritualists have a more difficult time explaining this phenomenon. Some reasons they have given for this are: (1) By attributing the messages to spirits, the messages carry more authority. The subconscious's statements therefore command more respect and obedience. (2) People like other people to make their decisions for them. By projecting their decision-making power into a foreign voice, they may relieve themselves of responsibility to some extent. (3) The "voice of spirits" is a tremendous attention-getting device. Thus your subconscious provides you not only with attention (and respect and power) when you work the Ouija, but also significant ego-satisfaction. (4) Finally, people *want* to believe in life after death. Having your subconscious answer your conscious questions in the voice of a dead spirit can thus be seen as pure wish-fulfillment.

We can't know for sure which, if any, of these reasons are correct until a lot more research has been done on the way the mind works.

A Ouija Sampling

To give you just a quick idea of the range of Ouija board experience, here are some brief stories.

Rudolf Friml, the noted composer, claimed he talked with several dead composers regularly via the Ouija board, among them Chopin and Victor Herbert. They occasionally dictated music to him. During World War II, Friml also talked with the spirits of Woodrow Wilson and Napoleon, who assured him that Germany was going to lose.

In Mexico, in 1910, Francisco Madero was told by his Ouija board that if he led a revolt, he would become the chief executive of the newly liberated nation. Madero, after some initial setbacks, succeeded in overthrowing Porfirio Diaz, and in 1911 he was elected President. (The Ouija board did not foresee his assassination two years later, as he was being taken to prison.)

One woman, when 17, was told by the Ouija board that her boyfriend, a soldier in Vietnam, had been shot at by another GI. The board was specific in its details: it was night, Gary was riding in a Jeep with another soldier, the flashlight Gary had been holding in his hand was hit, Gary had not been hurt. She wrote Gary about this, half-thinking she was crazy. But Gary, shocked, verified that the story was true. The details were accurate; he had been shot at— *while the letter was in transit.*

A 78-year-old woman worked with the Ouija board happily for thirty years. A horse-racing fan, she used the Ouija board to pick winners. Her greatest success came when the board told her to box three numbers—she won $768.

But in case you thought the Ouija board only told you things you wanted or ought to hear, here is a letter I received from the mother of a child who was traumatized by her Ouija experience.

> Just before our daughter's twelfth birthday four years ago, she played Ouija with her friends and asked the question, "When will I die?" The board answered, she told us, that she would die at age 13! My husband and I didn't think anything of it at first, not being superstitious and knowing that it was just a game.
>
> However, as time passed, we realized the impact that this "game" prediction had on our daughter. We eventually couldn't ignore the changes in her life, i.e., avoiding going out very far from home, dreading trips, taking illness like the common cold very seriously. Our daughter was very fearful, often speaking of her dread and crying many times. The tension was building in our family and we found *ourselves* becoming frightened for her *and* us, because she believed it so much.
>
> As her thirteenth birthday grew nearer, our daughter seemed more resigned and didn't talk about her fate as much as before—almost like the Kübler-Ross stages of Death and Dying—now Acceptance. We weren't sure what was happening, but on the day of her thirteenth birthday, she

boldly announced that she had fooled the Ouija game! We knew then that this fear had never left her, and frankly we, too, were relieved to see her reach age 13.

I am writing you about this experience because I thought you would be interested. I know this game has been around a long time, and I believe it is just that, a game. But apparently it can have some serious effects, especially on impressionable young people. This short letter may not reveal to you completely just how much effect our daughter's reaction to Ouija had on our family that one year. You would have to know the kind of people we are, and that feelings, like I have described here, haven't occurred to us before the game experience or since.

Similarly, I have heard of a happy, gregarious 11-year-old who suddenly turned into a terrified little child, afraid to leave her home, convinced she was about to be struck dead—all because of one particular session with the Ouija board. The quality of her schoolwork dropped from excellent to failing. She lost weight. She developed symptoms of paranoia. In desperation, her parents took her to a psychiatrist. Eventually, after a lot of visits, heartache and considerable expense, the psychiatrist was able to cure the child of the dread that had scarred her youth.

Both girls suffered from "mediumistic psychoses." More will be told about this in Chapter 13.

In addition to sending Ouija players to doctors, the board has also driven a number of people to some very strange behavior.

In 1920, an American sailor claimed his Ouija board told him that his wife's missing ring was taken by a friend. The sailor beat that friend. A judge determined that the Ouija's testimony did not justify assault.

In 1933, a teenage girl claimed that while working the Ouija board with her mother, she was instructed to murder her father, because her mother was in love with another man. The Ouija board supposedly gave the girl specific instructions and promised her $5,000 in insurance money and escape from the law. The girl was sent to state reform school for six years, and her mother was sent to prison to serve up to twenty-five years.

In 1935, a Ouija board told Mrs. Nellie Hurd in Kansas City that her 77-year-old husband, Herbert, had given $15,000 to a woman with whom he was having an affair. Mrs. Hurd began an intense program of husband abuse, systematically beating, burning and torturing him. Mr. Hurd could not convince her that the Ouija board was lying. In desperation he killed her.

In 1956, the last will and testament of heiress Helen Dow Peck provided that the bulk of her $180,000 legacy was to go to a certain John Gale Forbes. A judge invalidated the will. No John Gale Forbes could be found, for he was merely the creation or invention of Mrs. Dow Peck's Ouija board.

3

OUIJA VARIETIES

There are other phenomena, like the Ouija, about which spiritualists and believers of automatistic theory disagree. These include automatic writing, table-rapping, the pendulum and, to some extent, dowsing.

I bring them up now because of their similarity, and because some of the people discussed in this book experimented with a variety of Ouija-like devices and techniques.

Automatic Writing

Automatic writing occurs without the writer's conscious involvement. Although what is being written may be perfectly comprehensible, even brilliant, there is no conscious thought behind the ideas expressed; nor is the pen or pencil deliberately moved by the writer. A simple example of this can be found on the page of doodles one often unconsciously makes while talking on the telephone or sitting through a long meeting. Automatic writing is not a deliberate act, can occur spontaneously, and is usually done while the writer's consciousness is deliberately turned to an activity other than the automatic writing itself. It is also known as trance writing, when the writer is "entranced," or spirit writing, when the writer is in touch with spirits.

Wells, Huxley and Wells, in their book *Science of Life,*

describe automatic writing this way: "In these circumstances, the hand with the pencil may write not only voluminously, but often coherently and interestingly. What it writes would appear to be the product of some *system of ideas* which is denied full access to the normal main consciousness—more or less thoroughly dissociated, repressed, or buried."

A pencil is used more often than a pen for automatic writing simply because the soft lead of a pencil requires less consistent pressure than a pen to produce script. A planchette is sometimes used, with one of its three legs replaced by a pencil. Thus, when two people touch the "little table" together, they combine their psychic forces.

Some people can write automatically with both hands, each hand writing about different subjects. Sometimes the lines are written upside down or backward so that one needs a mirror in order to read what was written. There have even been cases where every other word was written backward, or where the whole page was written backward, starting at the bottom right-hand corner.

Automatic writing can proceed at feverish pitch. One person wrote in two minutes—very legibly—what another person needed twenty minutes to copy.

Practiced mediums write automatically more freely than beginners. Beginners often produce illegible writing or curious drawings. Their writing arms may swing wildly, even to the point of causing physical pain. It has been found that post-hypnotic suggestions work well in freeing beginners to write automatically.

The handwriting generated by the *autonographist* is usually different from his normal everyday writing. It's usually more cursive. Words and sentences are often linked and must be separated or punctuated after the automatic writing session is completed. (This is also the case with Ouija board dictation.) Words, sentences, paragraphs more often than not run together.

The style and content of automatic writing is also

different from one's normal everyday writing. In some cases, both the style and content are superior to what the writer can produce normally. Many automatic writers refuse to accept the idea that their automatic writing is their own work, subconscious or not; and they attribute the work to a personality or intelligence apart from themselves.

One aspect of automatic writing that encourages the idea of "the Other" doing the writing is how the autonographist can hold lengthy conversations while writing. Most often the automatic writer doesn't know what has been written until the writing is completed and he reads it for the first time. This delayed comprehension of the given, completed message is also true of Ouija board operators who can't understand their dictated messages until the dictation is completed and reviewed as a whole.

Stories of prophecy, telepathy, clairvoyance and contact with spirits abound. Reportedly, in the late nineteenth century, Horatio Hunt and James Burns regularly corresponded telepathically through automatic writing, though they lived three hundred miles apart.

Ouija board operators sometimes graduate to automatic writing. Automatic writing is faster, more immediate. It also has the advantage of being transcribed directly onto paper as it occurs, without the help of another person. Some automatic writers are able to switch from the pen or pencil to the even faster typewriter. In all cases, the exact nature of the events is hotly debated.

A Classic Case of Automatic Writing

A famous example of automatic writing and its often striking messages concerns the Glastonbury Abbey, a church in Great Britain. Like many ancient structures, even older structures had been built in the abbey's vicinity or incorporated into it. The Edgar Chapel, for example, was thought to have been completed no later than 1539; it had been destroyed and its exact location was unknown, with only scant references in ancient documents testifying to its existence. A second structure built later in the sixteenth century, the Loretto Chapel, had also been destroyed and lost.

In November 1907, a local architect, Bligh Bond, asked a friend of his, John Alleyne, to experiment with automatic writing. Doing so, the two men asked for information about the history of Glastonbury Abbey. The hand of Alleyne traced an outline of the main abbey building. The outline also included the exact location of the lost Edgar Chapel. The drawing was signed, "William the Monk."

At another automatic writing session, a second character, "Johannes Bryant," added even more detail about the lost chapel: its position, dimensions, depths beneath the earth, the number of pillars and windows. This "character" also predicted that the then newly formed Somerset Archaeological Society would name Bligh Bond the director of abbey excavations.

The prediction came true, and in 1908 Bond began excavating, knowing exactly where to begin the dig. After months of effort, it became clear that the location, size and shape of the newly revealed ruins of the Edgar Chapel coincided with the specific descriptions earlier received via the automatic writing.

But Bond, strongly suspecting that the neighborhood ecclesiastics would be prejudiced against his excavation methods, did not at that time mention the automatic writing in his official reports to the excavation committee in his parish.

World War I interrupted the work. But in 1919 Bond resumed digging at the Glastonbury site. This time he unearthed the Chapel of the Lady of Loretto in exactly the location indicated by the automatic writing.

At this point, Bond went public with the story. A scandal did follow, but despite the growing controversy, work was permitted to continue.

Then, in 1921, the location of a previously unknown Norman wali—exact site, architectural details, etc.—was indicated with the usual precision by the automatic writing. But the prejudice against Bond's methods (no matter how successful they were) created a tremendous international scandal and he was cut from his post unceremoniously!

Bond then traveled to the United States and did not return to Somerset and the Glastonbury site for many years. When he did at last return, it was only to find out that his archaeological work had been methodically undone.

The rediscovered walls of the extension of the Edgar Chapel had been re-covered with earth; some of the wall's stones had been removed and many location markings were ruined. Bond wrote to the London *Times:* "On my return from an absence of many years in America, I was dismayed to find that with the exception of the Loretto foundation, the whole of the remaining landmarks of my years of steady archaeological work had been either obliterated or else so altered by wrong surface markings as to make them unrecognizable."

The explanation given by those then in charge of the abbey was the desire "to improve the condition and appearance of the lawns by eliminating all that might obstruct the operations of the lawnmower." Perhaps it was felt that the use of automatic writing as an archaeological tool tainted the find.

Table-Turning

Table-turning, table-lifting, table-rapping, table-tilting and table levitation are all forms of Ouija-like automatism. The similarities are greatest when you consider the Ouija board's pointer or planchette as a "little table." The principle is the same; only the size of the table is different.

Here's how table-turning works. A group of operators seat themselves about a table, preferably a three-legged table. They place their hands flat on the tabletop. They wait, perhaps for some time, for the first hint of movement. Sometimes the table rotates, limited by the reach of the operators' arms. But sometimes the table moves across the room and the operators must rise and follow it. They may need to run in order to keep up with it. None in the group thinks he is causing the table to move.

In table-rapping, the experimenters ask the table questions. The table answers by rapping or tapping a leg or legs against the floor. The usual formula says that one rap is No, two is Yes. Sometimes the table answers by signaling each letter of the alphabet in code: one tap for A, two for B, etc. In this way the tapping table exhibits all the linguistic versatility of the Ouija board itself, although it is, of course, a clumsier, more time-consuming method.

Table-Rapping and the Rationalists

Table-rapping became extremely popular in the mid-1800s in North America, Great Britain, France, Germany, Turkey and China. Some of society's most important people were avid table-rappers. Michael Faraday, the great English chemist and physicist (1791–1867) thought it was getting out of hand and set out to explore the workings of table-rapping in a scientific manner. He gathered a group of avid table-rappers in his laboratory. He asked them to turn the table in their usual fashion. They did. The table answered questions in a coherent, sequential fashion. It jumped up and down. It walked across the room. It did all it was supposed to do. Sometimes one person alone worked the table, sometimes a group.

And Faraday observed. He was unable to detect any electrical or magnetic forces at play, no special forces. Still, he was personally convinced that the table-rappers themselves were causing the characteristic movements of the table.

He contrived and tested several experiments. He inserted glass rollers between two flat boards that rested on the tabletop. He then rigged a lever arrangement so that if the upper board moved to the left before the lower board did, an indicator made of reed leaned visibly to the right. This meant that if the operators exerted pressure on the table—not merely followed it as it went through its paces— the reed would lean to the right.

The experiment was held; the reed definitely leaned to the right. Faraday went on. He proved that it is difficult, if not impossible, to press *only* directly downward. The pressure from the hands is not precise, the hands will also press down obliquely.

Though Faraday believed in the operators' honesty, the fact of their unconscious manipulation of the table was made visible and undebatable. When the table-rappers saw that they indeed were causing the movement, their surprise was great. And suddenly they were no longer able to create table-rapping or -turning effects.

Faraday explained it thoroughly. "The power is gone; and this only because the parties are made conscious of what they are really doing mechanically, and so are unable to unwittingly deceive themselves."

Thus Faraday concluded his experiment. "I must bring this long description to a close. I am a little ashamed of it, for I think in the present age, and in this part of the world, it ought not to have been required."

But table-rapping did not die with Faraday's experiments. Far from it. People still practice this form of mediumship.

One devoted table-rapper was W. L. Mackenzie King, who was prime minister of Canada for twenty-one years. When Mackenzie King's private diaries were first made public in 1980, they created a sensation in Canada and internationally. They showed that for decades he had engaged in table-rapping and spirit chats with his deceased mother.

In 1948, Mackenzie King was in London, receiving

spirit messages from Franklin Delano Roosevelt (who died in 1945). Roosevelt advised King that he should not retire from public life. Roosevelt also said Mackenzie King possessed a wisdom greater than that of Winston Churchill; that Churchill would do well to take King's advice; and that he, the spirit of Roosevelt, would keep King updated on all events while King slept. When Mackenzie King sent Churchill the transcript of these messages, Churchill was not amused.

Pendulum

Although ancient, the pendulum is the simplest of all the Ouija-like forms. It, too, mysteriously moves without conscious control. It, too, moves because of subconscious muscular movements too subtle to be noticed by the operator.

The pendulum responds to your questions with Yes and No movements. The operator holds the string that has a weight attached to the end so that the weight dangles without movement. The operator must first concentrate on the word *yes*. Soon the pendulum will begin to swing either clockwise or counter-clockwise. From then on, that movement will mean *yes*. If *yes* is clockwise, *no* will be counter-clockwise. Questions can then be asked. The pendulum will answer.

Because the subconscious is usually the source of the pendulum's movement, working with the pendulum is an excellent way to deal with mixed or uncertain emotions. The pendulum can help you to understand what you really feel, not just what you consciously think you feel.

The pendulum is good for clearing up cloudy memories, locating lost objects and clarifying important personal decisions. Of all the automatisms, the pendulum is commonly thought to be the least dangerous, the least threatening.

By suspending a pendulum over an alphabet, one basically creates a new form of the Ouija board—a much more powerful instrument; also a much more dangerous one.

The pendulum can also be used for a search process called map-dowsing. In this case, the pendulum is used somewhat like a water witch or dowsing rod.

Here's how map-dowsing with a pendulum works. Simply hold the pendulum in the usual way above the appropriate map. Ask the pendulum to locate whatever it is you're looking for—buried ores or treasures, lost objects, etc.— and it will indicate an answer, pointing to a specific spot on the map in service. (One can achieve this same effect using the pointer or planchette; they are, after all, nothing more than varieties of the Ouija principle.)

And does map-dowsing work? Again that's controversial, but here's a starting point: Dr. J. Norman Emerson, president of the Canadian Archaeological Association and the head of the archaeology section at the University of Toronto, Ontario, is a pioneer in the use of psychic techniques in archaeological exploration as reported in *Psychic Archaeology*. Working closely with a psychometrist (that is, one who "reads" objects), and with map-dowsing, Dr. Emerson has successfully located dozens of ancient sites, all previously undiscovered, without having to leave the University of Toronto campus. Dr. Emerson's documented map-dowsing finds include the Black Creek site (Iroquois) in Toronto city limits and a seven-thousand-year-old Indian long house, with its original tools and carvings, in Parry Sound, north of Ontario province.

Using the same pendulum-and-chart (map-dowsing) technique, a Canadian government anthropologist, Dr. William Ross, reports a site-find success rate of 75 percent in the Arctic!

Dowsing

No one knows for sure why dowsing works . . . but work it does. Dowsing is primarily done to find water, but it is also done to find oil, minerals, treasure, etc. Supposedly it was used quite successfully in Vietnam to locate land mines.

The rod is traditionally a fork of hazel wood, though it can also be made of other materials such as iron or plastic. All the dowser does is take the rod and wait for it to signal him. The dowser is not supposed to move the rod consciously; in fact, he is supposed to try to keep the rod from moving. Yet the rod does move, suddenly and violently; at times pulling with such force that the hazel bark peels off and burns or blisters the restraining hands.

This seemingly independent movement of the rod usually convinces the diviner that the pulling force exists independent of himself. "There are two explanations as to how this works," wrote parapsychologist Alphonsus Trabold. "One is that the object itself gives off a special radiation that affects the dowser or rod directly. The other explanation is that the dowser locates the object through clairvoyance and that the subconscious mind then causes the rod to dip towards the ground."

James Trow, professor of geology at Michigan State University and a professional mineral prospector, has another theory. "When we're dowsing, we're finding an electric field," he explains. "There's just electricity in the ground, in the air and in us. Certainly it's nothing psychic."

OUIJA

AND THE HELPFUL VOICES

4

OUIJA AND
ITS FIRST LITERARY STAR

The Ouija board has made an impressive mark on the literary world. This simple piece of masonite with its plastic pointer is credited with either authoring, coauthoring or causing to be written tens of thousands of pages of published works.

One spectacular case began in Saint Louis on July 12, 1912. Emily G. Hutchings suggested to Pearl Curran that they "try something with the Ouija board." Pearl agreed, and together they visited a third neighbor and friend who pulled a Ouija board out of her closet. During that first session, they received a message supposedly dictated by a deceased relative of Emily.

Encouraged and intrigued, Emily purchased her own Ouija board and took it over to Pearl's; they continued their "curious experiments" with modest success until—two months later—Pearl's father died. For a while Pearl refused to have anything more to do with the "Mysterious Talking Oracle," but eventually Emily was able to convince her that the experiments were harmless. The sessions resumed. Over a period of months, the two neighbors received a series of messages from Emily's deceased mother, Pearl's recently deceased father and a variety of other spirit personalities.

Again Pearl became hesitant about the experiments.

Her husband was an avid churchgoer and opposed to anything "spiritualistic." Emily's husband, an agnostic, teased the women mercilessly.

Then came the vital turning point: On July 8, 1913, just four days short of a year since Pearl first sat at the Ouija board, a message came in a rush, whole and unequivocal. It was:

"Many moons ago I lived. Again I come. Patience Worth my name."

Astounded, the two women wrote the message down, and after a brief pause, yet another followed: "Wait, I would speak with thee. I make my bread at thy hearth. Good friends, let us be merrie. The time for work has passed. Let the tabby drowse and blink her wisdom to the firelog."

From the moment this unexpected guest first introduced herself, the words flowed from her. In five years she dictated four million words—epigrams, poems, allegories, short stories, plays and full-length novels. Her collected works fill twenty-nine bound volumes, 4,375 single-spaced pages, including thousands of pages of conversation.

No shrinking violet, Patience thrived on working in the midst of sympathetic visitors. There could be large numbers of people in the house, coming and going, old friends of Pearl as well as new friends. Patience would converse with these people, taking time off from her primary desire, to write. Her dictation leaped from composition to composition, from poetry to prose and back again, interspersed with personal spontaneous talk, greetings and good-byes to the visitors.

Pearl's guests often included the famous. Edgar Lee Masters "talked" with Patience at one session. "I am not prepared to give an opinion as to whether her stuff comes from Patience Worth," he replied afterwards. "There is no doubt, however, that she is producing remarkable literature."

Patience revealed little about her earlier life on earth. Over the years all she admitted was she was born in 1649, a poor girl bred and reared in the countryside near Dorsetshire, England. Minimally educated, she worked in the house and fields, striving always to do her jobs well. As a mature woman, she migrated to America; in 1694 she was slaughtered in an Indian raid. That's all she would say.

Until 1919 the words poured out of Patience in a dictated flood. "The Fool and the Lady" and "The Stranger" are short stories, both set in medieval England, as was a full-length play, *Redwing*. There were five full-length novels: *Telka, The Pot Upon the Wheel, Samuel Wheaton, Hope Trueblood, The Merry Tale*, and the most successful and popular of them all, *The Sorry Tale*.

The Sorry Tale, a 300,000-word novel about the earthly life of Jesus, was dictated letter by letter over a period of two years. There are more than two hundred characters in the novel, all of them expressed in narrative action, not merely superficially described. Full of "passion, humor, tragedy, meanness and moral splendor," the "Oriental detail of the narrative is amazingly lavish and vivid throughout," the critics said. The resolution of its intricate plot occurs only in the very end of the last chapter (6,000 words), which was dictated in a single evening, a composition of "appalling force."

This novel was a great popular and critical success. The reputable and unsensationally minded firm of Henry Holt published the book, and Henry Holt himself asked Patience what colors she would like on the cover. Patience requested the colors of the sunset, and Henry Holt consented. The reviews of the spirit-written book included some absolute raves:

> "This long and intricate tale of Jewish and Roman life during the time of Christ is constructed with the precision and accuracy of a master hand. It is a wonderful, a beautiful and a noble book" (*The New York Times,* July 8, 1917).

> W. T. Allison, professor of English literature at the University of Manitoba, wrote, "No book

has ever thrown such a clear light upon the manner of Jews and Romans in the Palestine of the day of our Lord" (*Winnipeg Globe,* September 21, 1917).

Dr. Roland Greene Usher, professor of history at Washington University, Saint Louis, said, "Unquestionably this is the greatest story penned of the life of Christ since the Gospels were finished. One leaves it with a sense of understanding much previously dark and vague" (*Reedy's Mirror,* June 19, 1917).

Patience's second novel, *Hope Trueblood,* is set with massive, vivid detail in the seventeenth century. It is the story of a self-reliant peasant girl living in an English village. Victimized by prideful men of superior wealth and education, Hope Trueblood eventually triumphs because of her own courage, intelligence and resolution.

The *New York Times* described the plot as being contrived with "skill, deftness and ingenuity, permeated with spiritual beauty." The Chicago *Mail* told its readers that they would "wonder at the sheer beauty of the story's thought and diction." The Los Angeles *Times* said, "One cannot escape the realization that here is a masterpiece. Can it be that this is some Bronte from spirit land who has found a tiny aperture through the bleak wall of death to which she has pressed her lips?"

Perhaps the most glowing review appeared in the New York *Tribune.* "Whether in the body or spirit, the author is singularly gifted with imagination, invention and power of expression. The psychological analysis and dramatic power displayed in the narrative are extraordinary and stamp it as a work approximating it as absolute genius."

Patience also wrote poems: about 2,500 in all. She won a national poetry contest in which forty thousand contestants submitted multiple entries. More important, though, Patience was regularly published in America's most prestigious annual poetry anthology. In *Braithwaite's Anthology of Poetry for 1917*, the poetry lover found three poems by Vachel Lindsay, three by Amy Lowell, one by Edgar Lee Masters and *five* by Patience Worth!

Patience's main literary benefactor was William Reedy, the publisher of *Reedy's Mirror* and a major force in the American literary world of the time. (He was on the award-selecting committee for the first Pulitzer Prize for poetry.) Reedy was a regular visitor at Pearl's house, and he said of her poems, "They contain passages of bewitching beauty, of rare high spirits, of pathos. It does not equal Shakespeare or Spenser. It is not so great as Chaucer. But if there be any intelligences communicating poems by Ouija board or otherwise. . . . it is good poetry, better poetry than we find in our magazines as a rule—poetry with a quality of its own."

Indeed, Patience's best-known poem still stands up well.

Patient God

> Ah, God, I have drunk unto the dregs,
> And flung the cup at Thee!
> The dust of crumbled righteousness
> Hath dried and soaked into itself
> E'en the drop I spilled to Bacchus,
> Whilst Thou, all-patient
> Sendest purple vintage for a later harvest.

Many of Patience's poems were written on demand, and people were amazed at her versatility and productivity. Only once was she nearly stumped. In response to a specific request, she demonstrated an unheard-of hesitation, a "clumsiness" not experienced before or afterward.

A group of women—some old friends; others visiting the Curran home for the first time—were sitting about as Patience dictated via Pearl's Ouija board. The usual feats were being unhesitatingly performed, when a newcomer observed how in all the English liturgy there was no poem genuinely suitable as a bedtime prayer for children. The standard prayer most commonly taught children was distinctly morbid.

> Now I lay me down to sleep,
> I pray Thee, Lord, my soul to keep.
> If I should die before I wake,
> I pray Thee, Lord, my soul to take.
>   Amen.

Could Patience come up with a better prayer?

Silence. This was so unlike Patience's usual ease of communication that those in the room began to be concerned.

After a long, uncomfortable pause, the planchette moved. Patience explained that the making of such a prayer would have to be "a work of extraordinary delicacy and difficulty" because it would mean having to choose "terms in all respects suitable to a babe."

The session then went on and ended, and the visitors went home without seeing any further reference to the unexpectedly difficult problem. Patience had failed to respond to the challenge.

Two months later Pearl sat at her Ouija board with her fingers resting upon the planchette in the usual manner. An observer later reported, "Mrs. Curran circled a long time until we finally remarked upon it. Patience said at last, 'Nay, I hae a task which be such a lovin' one I be a-feared o' it!'

"Then, as though she felt the need of the Father's help, she uttered, 'Let my throat sing a song that will fall as a dove's coo. Oh, make my throat dulcet, aye, and my words as the touch of sleep. Give me the tongue, aye, and the power of simplicity!' "

There was another long wait. The planchette moved hesitantly, incoherently. This passed and the poem came.

I, Thy Child forever, play
About Thy knees at close of day;
Within Thy arms I now shall creep
And learn Thy wisdom while I sleep.
                              Amen.

Patience's love of children had long been known—and in one of the most unusual of all Ouija stories, she seems to have been the only spirit to become a mother. One evening, while sitting before the Ouija board, Pearl was astonished to see the message from Patience spell itself out—advising her to adopt an orphan. Patience gave specific details about the ethnic heritage of the child, the child's physical attributes, and also where Pearl would find the child. Pearl discussed this message with her husband, who agreed that they should adopt. And after several months of searching, they found a daughter (Patience had been most emphatic about the child's sex) who matched Patience's description. The papers were drawn up, and Patience Worth Curran had a new mother— or two new mothers, if you included the 250-year-old spirit. Patience always considered herself the mother, often giving advice and talking to her daughter when she got older. Patience stipulated that the proceeds from her works should go to her daughter.

Pearl and Patience had an unusual relationship. For the most part they were friends, although when Pearl made corrections Patience didn't approve of, or when she would start to guess how words or sentences would end, Patience could be very caustic in her criticism.

Pearl did not consider herself a writer. She had only eight years of schooling and almost no knowledge of literature. She was not a Spiritualist and she said that she was not a medium.

When asked about the Ouija board, she replied that it

"is just a piece of dead wood, nothing more." She continued, "It is I who move the board, in response to the subconscious or conscious impulse. There is no mystery in the movement; the mystery, if any, is in the source of the impulse."

So who was Patience Worth? A discarnate spirit, long dead, speaking through the Ouija board? That's who Patience said she was. Or was she Pearl Curran's secondary personality? Both Patience and Pearl denied that interpretation.

In *Venture Inward,* Hugh Lynn Cayce wrote, "In most instances the result (of working the Ouija) is weariness and impatience and the discovery that the unconscious layer available through such techniques is of little help and frequently exceedingly dull. In a small percentage of instances, those who persist discover deeper levels from which come poetic prose or poetry and frequently a great many religious admonitions. Some few may break through to creative areas." Is this what happened to Pearl Curran?

The man in the best position to answer these questions was Dr. Walter Franklin Prince who, in his capacity as research officer for the American Society of Psychical Research, conducted several studies of the Patience Worth phenomenon. He witnessed several of Patience's sessions, and also interviewed Patience. Prince come to one firm conclusion: that Pearl was honest. No one could consciously fake Patience's writings and answers so quickly, so well. Patience's versatility and writing ability were genuine and astonishing.

On the larger question—the spiritualist versus the automatistic view of the Ouija—Prince hedged his answer. He concluded that we must either accept Patience Worth as a spirit, or as one of the most amazing phenomena to come from the human subconscious.

In 1922, when Pearl was 39 and pregnant with her first child, her husband—who had long since overcome his distaste and disbelief and enthusiastically acted as secretary— died after a long illness. Pearl's mother died shortly after that. Patience tried to comfort Pearl, but their communication decreased. Also, by the mid-1920's, interest in Patience was on the wane. Fewer of her works were published; fewer people bought them. Pearl died in 1937.

An interesting footnote to the story of Patience Worth: After it became clear that Patience's sole contact was Pearl, Mrs. Hutchings was independently contacted by other spirit voices, among them the spirit of Mark Twain. She got to be on a first-name basis with him, and he dictated to her a novel named *Jap Herron*. It was even published, although Harper & Brothers, the publishers of Mark Twain when he was alive, sued *Jap Herron*'s publisher, saying that the novel was not up to Twain's usual high standards. The court ruled that Twain's name could not appear in the book, although they ruled that Twain's likeness could appear on the frontispiece.

5

THE OUIJA, JANE ROBERTS AND THE CALLING OF SETH

The use of the Ouija board often leads to further paranormal experiences. Pearl Curran and the development of her psychic powers is a good example. By the end of 1919, she had abandoned the Ouija board for direct voice mediumship. Patience began speaking directly through Pearl's body, a radical evolution.

Pearl had developed the ability to anticipate—first slightly, then entirely—what the Ouija was going to dictate. After the great body of Patience Worth's literature was completed, the planchette increasingly failed Pearl. The pointer would do nothing more than circle aimlessly about the board.

But this was no great loss. For by that time, 1919, Pearl was not only able to anticipate what the Ouija board was going to say, but she was also developing the ability to see vivid mental pictures (clairvoyance) of the subject matters under discussion. Her psychic development was rapidly escalating. By February 1920, she was displaying direct voice mediumship—that is, Patience Worth was making actual use of Pearl's vocal cords, speaking aloud and directly through her.

This was a development that both Pearl and her husband welcomed. Neither interpreted the development from Ouija communication to trance mediumship as being a possession.

Jane Roberts has gone through a similar psychical evolution. The author of many best-selling books, including *The Coming of Seth* (earlier named *How to Develop Your ESP Powers*) and *The Seth Material,* Jane Roberts' personal history parallels Pearl's in many ways. Both began their psychical experimentation with a Ouija board. Both developed working relationships with their unexpected Ouija guests. Both worked with their boards with little profit for quite some time. Eventually, both women began anticipating Ouija messages, began visualizing images and evolved into various forms of trance mediumship. The only significant difference in the histories of their psychical development is that Jane Roberts evolved from Ouija psychism to trance mediumship faster than her predecessor. A life-changing relationship with the powerful "energy essence personality" that the world now knows as "Seth" quickly emerged.

Born in Saratoga Springs, New York, Jane attended Skidmore College and later had poems and short stories published in national magazines and literary quarterlies. Early in her career she wrote two novels, *The Rebellers* and *Bundu.*

Then she decided to write a book about ESP development. The only problem with the idea was that, at the time, Jane Roberts knew almost nothing about ESP, much less its development.

But she had heard of the Ouija board and decided to experiment. On December 2, 1963, she and her husband, Robert F. Butts, Jr., an artist, sat down with their newly purchased Ouija board and started their first experiments.

They felt very foolish but not for long. On their fourth try with the Ouija board, when they asked "Is there anybody there?" the planchette answered Yes. An essence calling itself "Frank Withers" introduced itself and said that he had most recently lived on earth as an English teacher; that both he and his wife, Ursula, had lived in Elmira, New York; and that he was born in 1885 and had died in 1942.

At their second Ouija board session, Frank returned and said that he had lived even earlier lives on earth. He said that, as a soldier in sixth-century Turkey, he had known both Jane and Robert. In fact, three hundred years earlier Jane had been the son of her present husband, and the three of them had been pals in Triev, Denmark.

The next session was pivotal. It was during the question-and-answer period that the essence calling itself Frank announced its proper and preferred name as "Seth," a name that better suited "the personality most clearly approximating the whole self I am, or am trying to be." He then revealed that there also existed better names for Jane and Robert. From that point on, "Jane" became "Ruburt" and "Robert" became "Joseph." Seth explained that both wife and husband had been associated with their newly revealed and assigned names, not in their present lives, but as higher existential points of their existences *as beings*.

As the Ouija board experiments regularly continued, vital changes were evolving. Jane began noticing that, even as questions were being asked of her Ouija board, answers were formulating themselves in her mind!

She was correctly and frequently anticipating answers. This initially panicked her, because she resisted the idea of being psychic. But, encouraged by her husband, Jane slowly began to accept what was happening to her. Soon she was the channel, the physical means through which Seth actually spoke.

By the end of January 1964, twenty Seth sessions had taken place and two hundred and thirty pages of typewritten manuscript had emerged. Since then, and from the very beginning, verbatim transcripts (usually written down by Robert) have been kept. These transcripts are the basis of Jane's books and articles, the foundation of her continuing research.

Since that first Ouija board session in 1963, Jane has had a variety of psychic adventures—automatic writing, seances and, most frequently, direct voice communication.

Now when Seth speaks in Jane's voice, facial expressions and body language change radically. Her voice becomes deep and powerful in a masculine way. Her face becomes something other than it ordinarily is; a man's appearance is superimposed over her feminine softness. Body language also becomes more masculine.

But Jane does not feel threatened by Seth; does not think or believe that there is, or ever has been, any attempt to displace her in her own body or possess her. Trance states are entirely voluntary in Jane's case. Seth never attempts to communicate through Jane while she's in a trance until she is both prepared and ready for trance communication.

This does not, however, mean that Jane never had doubts. She did. Many times she hesitated to continue experimenting. She often resisted her own inner acceptance of increasing psychic ability. For example, when she began to visualize images and sense that she was correctly anticipating Ouija messages before they were actually given, Jane realized that she was drifting into greater, more direct psychic phenomena. This was initially upsetting; she felt not so much fearful as doubtful. Where would it lead? Should she allow it to happen?

But Seth, as teacher, always prepared Jane. He was unfailingly considerate in educating her both intellectually and emotionally, one developmental step at a time. Seth, in fact, encouraged Jane to express her doubts, to take her time. This she always did, and she continued experimentation only when she felt fully prepared and positive about ongoing development.

The Seth experiments were not conducted in secret. Interested friends were and often are included in the meetings with Seth. Seth talks directly through Jane to visitors, answers questions, gives advice and openly carries on conversations and debates.

As for testing, Seth didn't have to prove himself to Jane. Jane knew, loved and accepted Seth. To ask him to prove himself would have been inappropriate. Occasionally, however, informal, playful tests were given to Seth. And even though they cannot be considered scientific, they were fascinating and conclusive insofar as those who witnessed them are concerned. One such test involved Seth's extremely detailed account of a returning friend's recent vacation trip. In that case, details known only to the vacationer and deliberately kept secret by him were recounted by Seth in minute detail and in correct sequence.

A particularly interesting experiment had to do with testing Seth's ESP powers. The test was conducted by Robert; when his wife was in a trance, he opened a closet filled with stacks of old newspapers, mostly back copies of the *New York Times.* He retrieved one section of a paper and, without looking at it, removed a single sheet. Held behind his back, it was folded and concealed in two previously readied envelopes. Seth, through Jane, then delivered himself of thirty-nine different impressions of that printed material. He described specific images, words and the page layout.

While the page was being blindly selected and placed unread in the double envelopes, Jane waited in a separate room, the door between the rooms closed. Only after Seth gave his impressions were the envelopes opened. The single page that had been blindly chosen by Robert was one from the *New York Times,* connected pages eleven and twelve, of the Sunday, November 6, 1966, edition. Of the thirty-nine impressions of the pages Seth had given, almost all of them had direct, affirmable application. This was an extraordinary score or "hit" response. It was typical of Seth's response under informal test conditions.

Through Jane, Seth has diagnosed illness, correctly described the contents of buildings and rooms many miles away and materialized as an apparition in well-lit settings. Considering himself a communicator and stimulator of thought, Seth has lectured on health, dreams, reincarnation, astral projection, the mechanics of humankind's subconscious and on the nature of God.

Why does Seth do all this? He says that he wants people to understand themselves better so they can reevaluate their understanding of reality and change it for the better. Working with Jane, Seth accomplishes this education by giving private and group instructions. But the primary means of teaching, at least in terms of numbers of people reached, is through Jane's books.

There the reader finds specific, step-by-step advice on the development of meditation techniques and ESP. This practical advice is combined with a great deal of philosophical and metaphysical speculation. But all the material relates to the individual's actual existence as an evolving entity whose understandings and ideas influence and change not only him or herself, but the whole of reality both immaterial and physical.

The Teachings of Seth

Through various incarnations, each person experiences a long period of training and learning. When incarnations on a physical plane are no longer necessary, the individual then evolves to other, higher planes of existence. Much greater developmental opportunities exist on these higher levels.

The basic lesson to be learned always has to do with karma or ethics. The crude individual learns to behave responsibly as various embodiments are experienced. Cruelty and hatred are returned, without exception. One literally gets what one gives. These hard lessons, once grasped, develop the individual spirituality. Once the spiritual development is adequate through as many incarnations as are necessary, the individual progresses to a much greater level of existence wherein godlike powers are made available.

But existence on the higher planes, and the use of the powers available there, are withheld until the individual has developed a finely tuned sense of ethical responsibility. Before the individual can progress, he or she must master all impulses to injure, control, exploit or destroy others. Until then, more incarnations, more training, more learning of the karmic lesson.

Once fully evolved, the individual is literally no longer a member of the human race. That is put behind. Now the liberated energy essence is most concerned with thoughts and emotions. These are instantly and automatically transformed into matter. Thought creates things; this is why the karmic reincarnational lessons must be taught and learned thoroughly.

The philosopher Immanuel Kant taught that the "mind imposes reality on the 'data' of the senses." Seth teaches a similar idea. His is that the senses themselves *and* ideas create material matter. An idea is an event is reality. All ideas impact our lives. Ideas profoundly impact the material world at all times. Understanding is broadened so that an enlightened consciousness can manifest itself in the real world. Denial of this merely delays the complete transformation of the physical world.

Seth uses the metaphor of all living human beings living in an isolated and soundproofed room. The lust on the part of individuals to control others in any way merely creates destruction in a closed system. Destruction thus creates more of itself; agonies multiply; they are sorely felt. There is no getting away from the pain of the hard lessons until the individual creates responsibility for self and stops trying to control others.

When the lust for the control of others is finally recognized as the completely destructive and hurt-creating influence that it is, responsible and broadened consciousness can flower. Until then, the pain, sorrow and agonies suffered within the closed room that is our world must continue, for the lessons of karmic responsibility for self would not be learned if the suffering were not both real and felt. Thus the parent spanking a child speaks more truth than is realized when he or she says, "This hurts me more than it does you."

The idea that the senses do nothing more than "take in" is an illusion, is false. The senses also create. They are far from being passive. Each sense creates, projects and focuses its "idea" onto the physical world. Each sense, in its own way, is a channel which creates physical reality.

6

THE POET AND THE OUIJA BOARD

Properties: A milk glass tabletop.
A blue-and-white cup from the Five & Ten.
Pencil, paper. Heavy cardboard sheet
Over which the letters A to Z
Spread in an arc, our covenant
With whom it would concern; also
The Arabic numerals, and YES and NO.
What more could a familiar spirit want?
Well, when he knew us better, he'd suggest
We prop a mirror in a facing chair.
Erect and gleaming, silver-hearted guest,
We saw each other in it. He saw us.

> from *The Book of Ephraim,*
> reprinted here with the kind permission of
> James Merrill.

Born in New York City, now living in Stonington,
Connecticut, Pulitzer Prize–winning James Merrill is
the creator of many books of poetry, novels and plays.
The Changing Light at Sandover is his lengthiest poetic
work, comprising three volumes that are a trilogy. His
"coauthor" in the making of the epic poem was the Ouija
board.

James Merrill began working with the Ouija board
because he had reached a point in his life where he wanted
to get beyond himself, to communicate with the "god"
within, or at least with a less familiar, less confined self that
would have greater vision.

The work began in 1953 when Merrill and a lifelong

friend, David Jackson, got good results with a Ouija board the first time they experimented with it. A story about an engineer "dead of cholera in Cairo" emerged; it was used in a short poem, "Voices from the Other World," the first piece Merrill wrote about the Ouija board. This poem was later incorporated into *The Changing Light at Sandover.*

Created over a period of many years, published in sections or books as they emerged, *The Changing Light at Sandover* is a masterwork more than five hundred pages in length. It includes *The Book of Ephraim, Mirabell's Books of Number* (which won Merrill's second National Book Award), *Scripts for the Pageant* and a coda, *The Higher Keys* (which won the National Book Critics' Circle Award). It was published in 1982 by Atheneum. Enjoying both popular and critical success, this wonderfully crafted poem take its readers on an adventure of discovery that is novel-like in its storytelling, scope and in the development of its main characters.

Sometimes tender, sometimes brutally frank, *The Changing Light at Sandover*'s characters, human and nonhuman, range across the surface of the planet Earth and throughout the cosmos. They evolve in their daily lives and beyond life on Earth, continually expanding, always revealing more about themselves and the writers.

The work addresses itself to the ultimate questions of origins and destiny. Although problems and conflicts of the characters in the poem are nicely resolved, one feels strongly that ultimate resolutions have somehow slipped away, leaving greater mysteries.

In a letter to me, James Merrill explains, "This may be a reason you find it hard to systematize the work. I should hate it if that were possible. What does come through again and again is that the 'truth' is self-revising—like any living organism, after all, a constant process of self-renovation."

Both David Jackson and James Merrill are characters in the trilogy. The "story" of the poem is, in part, a history of their experiences with the Ouija board, their travels to Europe with it, their use of it, their reactions to the personalities met via the board, etc.

Working together with the board, David Jackson is the subconscious receiver of the messages, the "Hand" as one of the poem's major spirit characters, Mirabell, describes him.

James Merrill is the poet or "Scribe" who shapes the messages in words and images. Both men's functions are essential to garnering the original Ouija board messages and making the poem a whole.

James Merrill is fully aware of the shared creativity of the process, and he sometimes feels that the work might well have been signed with both their names.

In addition to Merrill and Jackson, other characters in the poem include Jesus, Gautama, Mercury and Mohammed; the Angels of Light (Michael), Water (Emmanuel), Earth (Raphael) and Fire (Gabriel); the Nine Muses; and such notables as Maria Callas, Robert Lowell, Pythagoras, Plato, Gertrude Stein, Alice B. Toklas, Richard Wagner, W. B. Yeats, Ephraim; and some of James Merrill's and David Jackson's deceased friends and acquaintances, W. H. Auden, Maria Mitsotaki, George Cotzias and Robert Morse. All of these personalities and more communicate through the Ouija board, their observations and revelations incorporated into the body of the poem.

The many Ouija voices also include those of Wallace Stevens and Nefertiti. Once, quite unintentionally, Edna St. Vincent Millay suddenly appeared. She had been inadvertently mentioned just before a Ouija board session began and thought she had been summoned. It was an embarrassing moment for her—she wasn't used to the role of uninvited guest.

Are the Ouija board's voices, then, the authors of the poem? No, says Merrill, for two reasons. First, the trilogy as a whole does not entirely consist of verbatim transcriptions of the Ouija communication. There is a great deal in *The Changing Light at Sandover* that is pure James Merrill. Second, the Ouija communicators themselves insist that language, as such, is a human medium, not theirs. Merrill explains this in a Paris *Review* article (Summer 1982) written by J. D. McClatchy. Says Merrill, "It [language] doesn't exist . . . in that realm of cosmic forces, elemental processes, whom *we* then personify, or tame if you like, through the imagination. So, in a sense, all these figures are our creation, or mankind's. The powers they represent are real—as, say, gravity is 'real'—but they'd be invisible, inconceivable, if they'd never passed through our heads and clothed themselves out of the costume box they found there. *How* they appear depends on us, on the imaginer, and would have to vary wildly from culture to culture, or even temperament to temperament."

The poem, then, has a great deal to do with these relationships between human and cosmic forces. Furthermore, the experience and making of the trilogy in cooperation with the Ouija board allowed the poet to continue friendships with deceased friends in an ideal way. When they were alive, the relationships were, in part, determined by outside factors—the weather, for example, health, distances, etc. But with the Ouija board, the old friends and acquaintances were readily available without inconveniencing factors: each merely needed the others.

An important point is that, working with the Ouija board, the relationships with deceased friends continued to evolve, as did the poem itself, over a period of years. For example, James Merrill began working on the first part of the poem, *The Book of Ephraim,* only a day or two after his dear friend Maria Mitsotaki had died. He only mentioned her in that first book; however, in the second and third books, she evolved into a major character, important as much to Merrill as to the poem.

Of the earliest Ouija material, much had been lost and little had been transcribed. Merrill used what he could remember or had saved to shape *The Book of Ephraim.*

Much more had been transcribed and saved when Merrill started to write the second part of the trilogy, *Mirabell's Books of Number.* There he honed down two-thirds of the Ouija board material in shaping the final product. Before writing this book he had given up using the Ouija board for some time, picking it up again only because Jackson's mother was near death.

With *Scripts for the Pageant,* the third book, Merrill did very little editing. Except for small changes and decisions about structure, the material attributed to the Ouija board appears in the poem as it was originally dictated and transcribed.

Openly working with the Ouija board does not embarrass Merrill. And if his use of it embarrasses others, it's because, as the poet explains it, "they can't bear to face the random or trivial elements that coalesce, among others, to produce an 'elevated' thought." As far as Merrill is concerned, he is obliged during Ouija sessions to be a "well-tempered keyboard."

As for the Ouija transcriptions incorporated into the poem, Merrill describes the originals as looking like the compositions of children, all "drunken lines of capitals lurching across the page, gibberish" until punctuated and divided into words, sentences and paragraphs.

When working with their homemade Ouija board, David Jackson rests his right hand on the teacup used as a pointer, and James Merrill uses his left hand, freeing his right hand to transcribe. On average, the response is five hundred to six hundred words per hour. "Sometimes the powers take pity on us and slow down."

How much has the Ouija board contributed to the actual creation of the poem? The fact is that years ago, when the work began, Merrill had no idea where it was going. It evolved, and it did so organically through the Ouija communications, not forced at all by the poet or David Jackson. For example, Maria Mitsotaki came to play a large part in the work, but, as the poet says, "One would have to be a Jung or Dante to foresee her role in the poem."

But in addition to content, the Ouija board has influenced Merrill's style. Merrill's style often runs to couplets. He credits this to his psychic patron, Kinton Ford (1810–1843), who edited the works of the greatest English couplet writer, Alexander Pope.

Another characteristic of this particular Ouija board adventure is a high degree of good luck, events in daily life that, Merrill says, "kept staring me in the face." An example: A friend sent Merrill a joke about one of the poem's main characters, Ephraim, who, at a climactic moment in the poem, plays the role of host or emcee to an illustrious company of assembled characters. That joke became an unexpected part of the poem: "E—for Ephraim—equalling any emcee squared." This kind of good luck happened a great deal while *The Changing Light at Sandover* was being written; "I felt," Merrill puts it, "like a perfect magpie."

Merrill and Jackson also admit to having been frightened at times when the Ouija personalities took over. Merrill thinks it was because he and Jackson had *agreed* to the takeover "for the sake of the poem." There was something powerful and potentially dangerous there. Were they being possessed? Either the two men had had the strength to handle the experiences, or "we've been handled with kid gloves." These frightening experiences (visions; bodily transformations; felt, powerful presences) are vividly reported in the poem.

Some of their friends continue to be frightened for the

Ouija experimenters. One, more concerned than the rest, even took the poet to a Trappist monastery to talk with an understanding priest. Merrill read the Ouija transcripts and talked about the history of the sessions. "Afterwards, the priest admitted that they'd been warned in the seminary against these devilish devices, but that, frankly, I'd read nothing to him that he [the priest] didn't believe himself."

In a letter to me, Merrill wrote that he no longer recommends that friends use the board. "I've seen how it can sweep them up. One can never tell in advance how susceptible a given person will be. I suppose I'm more tough-minded than I knew. Or have been preserved by my two-mindedness, my mixture of joyous belief and amused skepticism, that kept waxing and waning over the years."

7

THOMAS, THE WISE OLD MAN IN THE SKY

Ruth-Ann Campbell—wife, mother and business-woman—is another of those fortunate few whose life has dramatically changed for the better because of the Ouija board. Once guilt-ridden and confused, she now understands that each day is an adventure meant to be fully celebrated. Instead of floundering in confusion, she now understands the connectedness of things. Events, ideas and people that used to upset her are now sources of meaning and inspiration. Her newfound knowledge fills her with courage and confidence. Healthy, busy and caring, Ruth-Ann knows who she is and likes what she knows.

Her life-changing voyage of self-discovery began back in her hometown of Mount Albert, Ontario, Canada. In 1973 she and her husband Dick began experimenting with a homemade Ouija board. "I was in a complicated period of my life. I had questions that needed answers. Years before, Dick had successfully used the glass and letters (a homemade Ouija) and suggested that we try it."

It was a very slow process. They experimented with friends, but found that they made better progress when they worked only with each other. Even then, nothing substantial happened; but they felt strongly that something good and positive, however vague, was developing.

Two years later, on a board they picked up at a garage sale, they made contact with Dick's deceased parents and a

51

spirit personality named Pat. Impatient for information and encouraged by the board's responsiveness, Ruth-Ann started working on her own. Suddenly the responses were swift and coherent. She was able to ask questions and get intelligent replies. She didn't run into any kind of gibberish or nonsense.

Although pleased with the improvement of her Ouija communications, Ruth-Ann began feeling increasingly frustrated with having to stop to write answers down. At that point, however, Thomas, a new board personality, came through. He had the surprising solution to that frustration.

"Meeting Thomas that first time was a highly emotional experience—exciting, joyful, loving. I felt myself responding wonderfully to this 'person.' Even the movement of the pointer was different.

"One day I was sitting with a pen in my hand, and suddenly the pen just started writing without my controlling it. It was Thomas expressing himself directly with the pen rather than the pointer. He wrote, 'You are a good and faithful person, and you have a mission to do. More later.' "

In the weeks that followed, Ruth-Ann and Thomas developed an especially close relationship. She was constantly amazed by his understanding of her, by his insights into her psyche. But she learned that theirs was not a new relationship. Thomas was someone she had known before—in other lives. She discussed the Thomas phenomenon in an interview with me.

"Thomas was my husband in my last life and in a number of other lives. We've also had other relationships, too—father, child, et cetera. It seems we go back a long way.

"When contact was made through the board and in the first few times of automatic writing, Thomas first used the name 'Wom.' Later, when he had explained our past relationships in other lives and, in particular, my immediate past life in which I had known him as 'Thomas,' he said we should address each other as we had known ourselves to facilitate establishing our new relationship. So Thomas always addressed me as 'Lady Lea' except when he's being stern with me, and then he calls me Ruth-Ann. When I think of Thomas as 'Thomas,' I picture him as my compatriot in work. When I think of him as 'Wom,' I see him as a composite of his total universal self.

"Now Thomas is like a part of our family. My husband, Dick, accepted him readily after the initial, ah [laugh] shock. As for Thomas, he thinks my husband is a wonderful person; that it was my husband who helped me to be content enough to allow Thomas to come through in the first place."

"I understand your parents were Fundamentalist missionaries."

"Yes, but even as a child I felt instinctively that something was wrong with that approach to life. Because I grew up in a Fundamentalist environment, I always felt guilty. I felt I was sinful.

"Thomas helped me and my family realize what life is all about. He's helped us become content. He's given meaning to what the world is and what everybody is going through. Learning about reincarnation, that was something very important. It explains a great deal.

"I now feel very confident about my place in life. I feel that everything I have lived and what I will be in the future has meaning, no matter what happens. I love life. And I have absolutely no fear of death. I'd describe myself as a joyful person. I'm happy."

"Dr. Anite Muhl, a psychiatrist who knows a great deal about automatic writing, says that it can reveal hidden or latent talents. Is that true in your life?"

"Yes. Thomas and I are writing a book, and he's helped me develop my writing ability. It took him a long time to get me to the point where I would actually sit down and start writing."

"What is the Thomas material about?"

"Love. The history of the world. The history of the Ouija board. How to use it. Why to use it. The planets; how they affect us. A little like astrology, but not really. It's kind of a background for someone getting into astrology. There's a good deal of material on dreams. And Thomas gives very specific instructions in a very practical way on how to communicate with his level of existence or intelligence, whatever you want to call it."

"What does Thomas say about the Ouija board?"

"That you must prepare yourself before you use it. You should say a prayer of protection. Your intentions should be good, that sort of thing. In this way you avoid getting yourself into trouble."

"Sir Arthur Conan Doyle and his friend Sir Oliver Lodge were very involved with spiritualism. Now, I haven't been able to verify it, but I was once told that they thought that the religion of the twentieth century would evolve from the Ouija board; that from it would evolve philosophical views that have more to do with reality as our time understands it than do the traditional religions."

"Well, that's very interesting because, really, Thomas and I believe that there does seem to be a psychic awakening in this age. People are going to have a different kind of religion. Their attitudes toward life are going to be different, so that's right."

"Please give me some details about the mechanics of your automatic writing."

"Initially it was very slow and laborious. The letters formed, however, into very neat and precise words. In the first two or three sessions the words did more or less run into each other. Such things as crossing the 't' involved a long line back and forth. At that point I didn't want to do anything that would seem to interfere with the process. As I became more interested in *what was being said* rather than the happening itself, I made a conscious effort to lift the pen when I could see that a word was finished. Even in the first efforts, the spelling, grammar, construction of sentences and punctuation were all there, and, yes, capitals too. I have never had to change or correct one thing Thomas has written. As I go back and reread notes from the early period, I do notice a change in style. The first notes seem to me much more old-fashioned, whereas today Thomas uses a more current style of vocabulary and idioms."

"When you work with Thomas, do you ask questions or does he come in and pick up where he left off?"

"It can be either way. Sometimes I have asked him specific questions and he just goes merrily on his way and writes about something else. Then, when I'm not expecting it at all, he'll say, 'Oh, by the way . . .' and he'll come through. But there are times I ask him a specific question and he answers right away. Other times he'll say, 'I'm going to do some research on it and get back to you later.''

"Ruth Montgomery does all her trance work with a typewriter."

"I asked Thomas if he couldn't please do that because I have to type up all my notes. But he says he doesn't feel too comfortable with the typewriter."

"What does Thomas look like?"

"In his last life he was medium height, dark, fairly long hair and a heavy scar across his face. He was a soldier. Now he looks like a . . . well, the family calls him The Wise Old Man in the Sky."

"Could you allow me to get in touch with Thomas?"

"I think he'd like to talk with you."

Conversation with the Wise Old Man in the Sky

THOMAS: I greet you, Stoker, as a friend. I am most happy to be able to send some thoughts your way via the hand of Ruth-Ann. I would now also like to express to you that I am in complete accord with your using any material that comes from myself or Ruth-Ann.

All Universal Truths are for sharing and learning. Each soul's contribution forms part of a whole scheme—a master plan. I, Thomas, and my compatriots are deeply involved in helping to get the knowledge of *all that is and true realities* into the conscious mind of mankind.

"Thank you. What is the Ouija board, Thomas, and what is the best way to work with it?"

The Ouija board is primarily a visible tool for invisible thought exchange. It is simply an instrument that facilitates receiving impulses, through the fingertips, of thoughts and impressions received by a person's mind. Thus it is not the board itself that is empowered in some magical way, but rather it is the user of the board who is the source of the power.

However, once a board has been used by an individual, there are vibrations that remain impregnated in the board and in the pointer. So it is advisable for each board to have one owner in order to avoid any crosscurrents. If an old board is used, at least a new pointer would be a good idea.

Both hands should be used with the Ouija board; one is placed in a resting position on the board and the other used with one or two fingers on the pointer. This creates a good energy flow. Other practical points are that the choice of the time for using the Ouija board should be a time of quiet and relaxation and also a time when you have a feeling of high energy output. Particularly for a person's first efforts at such mental activity do I recommend this.

Now, the use of the Ouija board to make contact with others who live at a non-earthly level requires some "spiritual" preparation. This means recognizing that an individual is made up of more than a physical body; that a soul's inner self is the integral part of a person's "wholeness." It is this inner self that brings you to the point of desiring to make contact with other levels of life. Thus I recommend the repetition of a prayer once the hands are in place on the board—either aloud or mentally. It can be of your own form or can be the following: "Oh God, Keeper of the Universe, I release my mind to the flow of the power of the universe. I desire only good that I may learn and develop. Protect me from any negative forces and surround me with pure love."

Now there is a surge of power and the pointer moves. Where are the messages coming from? It is usually a soul known to you in this life or another who has a strong bond with you. Any questions you might have need only to be thought, and they are received by your friend. Look for shortcuts and abbreviations, however, that will facilitate getting the "idea" to you of what your friend wishes to say.

You may stop and record on paper what you receive, or you may speak aloud into a recorder. Neither will detract from or break the contact.

"How did the Ouija board come into use?"

As long as mankind has had written languages, the Ouija board has been in existence—particularly within the cultures using the cuneiform type of system. This present age of great mental awakening and awareness has seen the Ouija and its use become almost common knowledge. But now its meaning and use is becoming void of the mystery and connotation of evil that has surrounded it in the past. As the Dark Age of religion is slowly losing its grip and the church leaders are no longer able to keep so many people's minds fettered, we are seeing the results of great efforts and work by many souls at all levels of life. Realizing the great potential with the simplicity and availability of the

Ouija board, there has been a particular group from my level of life who have concentrated great power in helping individuals seek out this form of mental thought exchange.

"Many people think that the use of the Ouija board is dangerous. What, if any, are the dangers?"

Capriciousness and maliciousness exist on all levels of life that lie beneath the perfection of soul that we call "God." And in the area of communication via a Ouija board, it is certainly possible for these emotions to be expressed. This is why I have always stressed how vital it is for a person to be prepared for such communications. Those who use a Ouija board as a game, those who are totally ignorant of what is involved, those who are not always themselves governed by love can and do often leave themselves open to base emotions.

However, as within all the aspects of human life and living and its emotions, one does not say that something is wrong because of possible imperfections. The institution of marriage is not considered evil because there are bad marriages. Neither should a Ouija board be considered evil because of bad contacts. The central philosophy must always come back to the preparation, intent and aspirations of the user of the board. A person should judge his or her own basic strength of character and purity of love.

Examples of wrongdoings with the board are more usually brought to the light and remembered more easily than the good that has been accomplished with its use. But most souls know that *goodness* still outweighs all other facts of life.

"Thomas, will you tell me more about 'Wom'?"

My universal name, "Wom," means "A Soul with Much Love for His Fellowmen." Thus, much is explained about my pre-self self and my work with Ruth-Ann. When I was first able to break the barriers between our two worlds, I so identified myself because the sounds and vibrations of these "call letters" set up and kept open a channel between my mind and that of Ruth-Ann. The use of "Thomas" and "Lady Lea" came about because the relationships that Ruth-Ann and I have had in past lives made it more natural to so address each other. It did not then seem like a "super-being" was speaking to an "earthling," but rather that we were compatriots working together. The communication with Ruth-Ann is part and parcel of a much larger project. We were chosen and yet volunteers. We are part of a larger plan and yet our own efforts are as individuals. There are countless souls involved in this master plan, each with their own pet projects, their particular talents, their particular emphases. The advancement of spiritual knowledge and understanding at *all* levels is the basic premise for all of us.

I returned to the earthly plane in order to communicate with Ruth-Ann. I have many others that I consult with here and I also return to a higher level where I am refreshed because it is less cluttered with the problems of physical life. This level is an Ivory Tower, in a way; but for purity of thought, this level is vital.

Ruth-Ann and I had decided to work together *before* she returned to her present life. It took longer than we had planned to get in touch because this reincarnation beset her with many problems.

"Tell me, Thomas, how do you describe death?"

The "personality" of every soul is a composite of past, present and future forms. A baby that has grown to adulthood one does not say has died. The complexity of a soul must be understood in relationship to "time." Time as it is known on earth must exist for society to function. But there is truly no past, present or future within the framework of *true reality*.

The present-day writings having to do with what are called near-death experiences are quite accurate. These books in themselves are part of the knowledge being sent to this advanced age of mental awareness. The importance of knowing what to expect when one's soul leaves its body is to facilitate a quick and joyous transition from the earthly plane.

"What then is the best way to prepare for death?"

The best way to prepare for death is to study and accept the knowledge of reincarnation. With this comes the understanding of the reality of life, the totality of one's soul and the reasons for the interplay between other souls. This reinforces the rightfulness of communications from the earthly plane to a higher level, as this opens the door for participating in such learnings and teachings. Death should be looked upon as a glorious beginning and a joyous happening.

Stoker, my blessings I bestow on you all.

Conversation with Ruth-Ann, Resumed

"Have you personally ever had any trouble with the Ouija board?"

"Once. I got into contact with what you might call an evil spirit. But I'm glad it happened, because I learned something about it, learned something about myself. It was someone who obviously wanted to hurt me.

"Dick and I were visiting another couple, in their home. We told them about the experiences with the Ouija board. They were curious and wanted to try, but one of them was skeptical, very mocking and negative. On sitting down, the pointer would go only to NO—over and over again. Finally, it moved right to the edge of the table and would have fallen off. Stubbornly I insisted we could do better than that and persisted. Suddenly, the pointer did take off, but to my horror spelled out the message that my father had died! Actually, he was in the hospital at the time, on the other side of the continent, and very ill. I asked questions of the spirit for proof and identity. All the answers were correct. Well, greatly agitated, I stopped and phoned my father's room at the hospital. Who answered? He did! He even said he was feeling a lot better. The spirit had lied.

"It was many, many weeks before Dick and I would use the Ouija board again. The incident stayed constantly in my mind. I always came back to the thought that all other communications had been good—the positive far outweighed the negative. I realized that I really controlled the board—because all I had to do was stop.

"I shared these feelings with Dick, and eventually we decided to try the board once more before giving up completely. Thomas was still unknown to us and I had no guidelines, but I knew that I was praying for success and positive happenings. The session *was* good, our faith was completely restored and since then [about eight years] we have never had another bad contact.

"When contact with Thomas was made, one of my first questions to him was for an explanation of that incident. He said, 'You, Ruth-Ann, and your friend were not ready for communication that day. Through your ignorance, you had left yourself completely open and vulnerable. The spirit who "read your mind" tried to upset you with news of your father's death. There was an intent to hurt and also to dissuade you from your search for knowledge. This soul knew that I was waiting to get through to you. However, you learned a good lesson and did not give up. So, in looking back, it was a good experience for you. When you did return to the board, we on this side were ready and stood by you to make sure the channel was open to the right level.' "

"Ruth-Ann, did you ever wonder if you were really communicating with yourself through a fiction named 'Thomas'?"

"I wondered that, yes. In fact, one day I looked at the notes I had just received and I thought they were starting to look a lot like my own writing. This upset me considerably, as my first thought was, 'Don't tell me this is just something from my own imagination.' Also, I had been noticing that I was starting to anticipate what flowed from the pen. As

Thomas explained it to me, the writing was becoming swifter and looking more like mine because we were achieving a good balance between the thought exchange and the actual mechanics of transferring the thought to the mind, the brain, and out through the fingertips. I accepted this and stopped worrying about the 'look' of things."

"How long does a typical automatic-writing session last?"

"When we first started, we had many marathon sessions lasting up to two hours. This was when he was filling me in on details of our past lives together, and it seemed that he could go on forever. I found these sessions quite tiring, and my arm would literally ache. Once he started dictating the various sections of the manuscript, we settled into a routine of about an hour per morning, five days a week."

"What about predictions? Does Thomas make predictions?"

"No, nor have I verified facts about previous incarnations. It's just not an issue to me. A number of times Thomas has tried to forewarn us of a personal crisis or a good event. Such predictions have always seemed like oracles to me. It hasn't been until after the event we were able to interpret his remarks.

"Here's a story that offers some outside proof. Once Thomas received a message from a young man who had been killed in a car accident by a drunk driver. He asked Thomas to communicate to his mother that she should not grieve so much; that he was fine and her grief was keeping him bound to the earthly plane. Thomas said to me, 'Tell her this, and she will know that it is her son that speaks to her: "Mother, what did you find under my bed when I was a small boy? If you can say it was a box with a living creature in it, then you will know for sure who sends you this message." '

"I was reluctant to go see this woman, as this was a new experience for me and I was apprehensive as to what her reaction would be. I knew her only casually. Well, her reaction was total belief. She said her son had once hidden a squirrel under his bed and she had been very upset with him!

"I myself have often wished for some great, earth-shattering piece of proof. However, when I get this feeling I just remind myself to look at my notes. What greater proof could there be of my contact with another level of consciousness? He has helped me too much for me to doubt him!"

Ruth-Ann Campbell's spirit guide, Thomas, once told this story of the first Ouija board.

"It was in early medieval England that it came to pass that the use of 'letters' and 'tool' first came into use for communications between physical and spiritual entities. A group of monks were seated at a large table where they had partaken of food. As they sat and discussed the form of man as a soul, one member of the group happened to rest his hand upon an overturned drinking vessel. This gentleman, Gregory John, felt an almost imperceptible movement. Then as he looked upon the vessel and his hand, the vessel slowly started moving in a circle. Without a word from him, the group was instantly aware of the vibrations and all turned to watch this phenomenon. One, by the name of Paul, spoke up saying it was surely a sign from heaven and that they were being visited by some saint. After the first movement the cup had stopped. Now with this remark it again moved in a circular movement and stopped once more. Then Gregory remarked that he could feel a strong power through his hand and suggested asking questions as if to another being. Again there was movement. And so questions that could be answered Yes or No were rewarded with a circular motion to the left or right.

"As these were men gifted with the skills of language, they soon figured out that word-forming letters would mean more in-depth communication. The monks did not share this knowledge, however, for many years until they were one day directed to do so. This knowledge thus gradually spread to other monastic groups and finally into the public domain.

"This I tell you because it is part of the history of communication for the earth's time as you know or conceive of it, and because it is part of the Western World's heritage."

OUIJA

AND THE VOICES OF DANGER

8

OUIJA RAPE AND DEMONOLOGY

Please don't run out and buy a Ouija board because of Seth and Thomas or Patience Worth and James Merrill. Not every unexpected guest brings fame, money, joy or literary talent into the life of the Ouija-boarder. Not hardly.

What follows is part of a letter from a 28-year-old Colorado woman. She's a homemaker—mother of two and wife of an army officer. She has had a number of psychic experiences and had been a frequent user of the Ouija board.

"I desperately need help. I really have no idea how to explain the unexplainable to you. The unthinkable is happening to me. It is happening now as I attempt to write this letter. I will try to be coherent, logical and calm. I will try to give you the facts as best I can and hope that you can help me. I don't know where else to turn.

"I was a card reader and psychic all my life. Four years ago I made the devastating mistake of attempting to reach my deceased mother through the Ouija board. I got results, but it was not my mother whom I contacted. It was some sort of entity which had watched me since her death. I don't know what it is, but I know it is not human.

"The human spirits who used to help me with my work have disappeared. All there is now is *it*. My life is being dominated by this demon. Dear God, how can I tell you! Every day it viciously rapes, sodomizes and beats me.

"On the day it first came through the Ouija board, it pretended to be my mother. Later, I was automatic writing; and then suddenly, alone in my room, I was attacked. I am a married woman, but the pain of the assault was excruciating! I was afraid to cry out for fear that it would hurt my children who were in the next room. But it doesn't want my children. It is not interested in children, thank God! When it was done with me that first time, I needed medical care for the pain and for pelvic and bladder infections.

"Now I am virtually bedridden and in constant pain. It has not stopped torturing me since that first day. Violent beatings, stabbings, constant rape, that's all this demon does to me.

"My body is no longer the same. It doesn't function as it used to. You may think that I'm mad. I think I must be by now. It does all it can to force me to commit suicide! Constant badgering and berating. Verbal abuse so foul and sickening and dirty it is unbelievable! It is always covering me, hanging onto me, hurting, hurting, hurting. My husband often finds me on the floor or hiding or screaming so loud I'm afraid I might be carted out!

"It wakes me up—when it lets me sleep!—to rape and torture me. It is always there! Always there! Has this ever happened to any other woman?!

"I truly don't know where to turn! For some reason this foul and hideous thing has decided to help itself to my life! Please help me. I can't hold on much longer. It calls itself Sheikh Abdullah and speaks in a heavy Arabic accent. It has pretended to be many people and can make a voice like my mother's. It creates illusions and terrible, terrible visions, anything ugly it can add while it rapes and beats me.

"I feel more than half dead. Please, please help me."

This letter was not written to me, but to Ed and Lorraine Warren. Lorraine is a gifted psychic and Ed is a demonologist. They devote their lives to helping people like the young woman who wrote this letter—people who suffer the incredible torment of what the Warrens call spirit and demon possession.

The Warrens are, with Gerand D. Brittle, the authors of *The Demonologist*. In his introduction to their book, the Reverend John C. Hughes, a Catholic priest, describes the Warrens as a "compassionate, devout, loving, realistic couple devoted to fighting for the victims of demonic attack." He describes their work as "a holy and worthy aspiration and a serious career."

I spoke to the Warrens about the Ouija board. I asked Ed, ***"Would you and Lorraine ever recommend its use?"***

"No, no, we would not! Remember, I'm not just a psychic researcher, I'm a religious demonologist. The Ouija board opens the doors to the supernatural, to supernatural attack. When you use the Ouija board, you're communicating with an invisible, intangible realm, and negative spirits can enter through the board.

"Right now Lorraine and I are working on six devastating cases from across the United States and one in Canada, with what is called incubus attacks. The letter I just shared with you is an example."

"An incubus is an evil spirit or demon that rapes women."

"Right, and a succubus assaults men sexually. Four of our seven current cases entered the victims' lives via the Ouija board. My belief is that the only way these victims can be helped is through the rites of a religious exorcism."

"Does that mean you'll exorcise them?"

"No. I am not pious enough. My job is to evaluate such cases and then bring them to the attention of the proper authorities. If the victim is an Episcopalian, I take that person to the Episcopal Church. If Catholic, to a priest; if Jewish, to a rabbi. Only a fully ordained, very pious person can exorcise.

"Very shortly, Lorraine and I will be leaving for London and taking three people with us. We're going to see Reverend Christopher Neal-Smith, an Anglican cleric. He is probably the best-known exorcist in the western world, certainly England's most famous. He's a humble, pious man."

"But why all the way to England? Why not the church around the corner?"

"It's unfortunate, but in the United States we have to go through a lot of red tape to get help for the poor victims. It takes three or four years before the Catholic Church will even take notice of them! Besides, the Reverend Neal-Smith is not only willing to exorcise, but he can discern. By 'discern,' I mean that he can clairvisually and clairaudiently acknowledge what is there, the presence of a spirit if one is present. He can identify the problem immediately. Sometimes this kind of assault or possession is easily confused with psychosis. But these assaults are different from psychosis. Most of these suffering people have already spent years in psychoanalysis or had psychiatric treatment before they came to us. They've tried psychiatry—but it hasn't helped. Lorraine and I, we look for little clues, clues that tell us whether there's something preternatural afoot. We're like good fishermen who have to know when there's a fish at the end of a line even though we can't see it."

"These Ouija board obsession and possession cases: people being assaulted, raped by spirits or whatall, are they frequent?"

"Not uncommon. And the incubus cases are the most difficult. About eight months ago we had a young lady who was being constantly sexually and physically attacked by an incubus. We took her to a monastery in Georgia where monks constantly said prayers of exorcism over her. This provided her much-needed relief, and eventually she transferred to a convent."

"What about the letter you just shared with me?"

"It's one of many, Stoker. For some reason, there's an increase of this kind of case right now. And I'd say about seventy-five percent of our cases come from working with the Ouija board."

"But she said that she was automatic writing when the first attack took place."

"Right, but the demon made its first appearance when she was working with the board. The demonic spirits pick the time and place for an attack. You could use the Ouija board today and nothing supernatural may happen, but later—no telling when—the demonic may intrude on your life.

"I'm not saying that everyone who works with a Ouija board is going to be suddenly possessed. But possession, obsession, demonic assault—these things seem to occur when the Ouija board is used many times. Then the entities come through. When I say 'come through,' I mean through the free will of the Ouija board operator. That must be the case in every situation; the evil enters only when the victim invites it in through their own free will. The demonic has to be invited in."

"Have you ever been in contact with the board's manufacturer?"

"No, but I've been disavowing the Ouija board for many years, and our efforts haven't been in vain. Many people say to us, 'I've had a Ouija board for ages, but now that I've heard you talk, your different case histories, I'm going to get rid of it immediately!' "

"You and Lorraine must feel very secure within yourselves to be able to do your work."

"Yes, we do feel secure. People often ask us, if all the

terrible things we talk about actually happen, how is it we are still alive.

"Actually, Lorraine and I have been psychically attacked many times. And we've both been physically attacked by the possessed. But as a Catholic I have great faith in Jesus, in Saint Michael the Archangel and in the Blessed Virgin Mary. This faith is effective. Lorraine, too; her security lies in her faith. And the faith that she draws on gives me strength, too."

"Ed, how did you first become involved in this kind of work and research?"

"I lived in a haunted house as a little boy, from the ages of about five to twelve. My father was a very stern man, an officer in the Connecticut State Police, and he forbade us to talk about it outside the house. He would say, 'There is a logical explanation for everything that is happening in this home!' But he never came up with that logical explanation. After Lorraine and I were married, we traveled a lot. And whenever we heard about anything preternatural or supernatural, we'd investigate it. During that period we acquired much of the knowledge necessary for the work we do today. We didn't get our information out of textbooks. We actually went into troubled homes, hundreds of houses said to be haunted. I wanted to see if the things that had happened to me as a boy were happening in other homes.

"At some point it dawned on me that these people needed help and weren't getting it. They attracted psychic researchers and parapsychologists, but those people would only walk into their houses, look around, record the phenomena and then walk out. They left the people with demonic problems behind, still agonizing.

"I thought back to my early training as a boy in Catholic school. I wasn't a pious, religious kid by any means. In fact, I did everything I could to get out of going to church. But I got to thinking about the things the nuns and priests used to talk about. They had told me that I'd have a devil on my left and an angel on my right all my life, both telling me different things to do. Of course, as a boy, I simply dismissed it when they taught me about the devil and such. I didn't give what they had to say much credit. Now, after having been involved with demonology for thirty-seven years, I know these good people were quite right. There are physical, tangible forces that we come up against, forces that are much more than simple expressions of psychokinetic energy."

At this point Lorraine joined us and the conversation shifted.

"Lorraine, I'm now reading the work of Jane Roberts. She worked initially with the Ouija board, and it was through the Ouija that she first met her spirit guide, Seth, and their relationship seems benign."

"I don't know that I would call that benign! That was her evaluation."

"Well, Jane considers the Ouija board a positive instrument and openly advocates its use as a means by which one can develop psychic abilities."

"I know, but Ed and I have been involved in the research aspect of this work for a long while and Jane Roberts has not. We've spent a lot of time on the college lecture circuit, so we've met with a great many young people who find themselves in terrible possession situations. If people saw one-tenth of what we've seen, they wouldn't be so gullible."

"But Jane Roberts—"

"I'm sorry. I don't really believe that most mediums know what is coming through the board. They may believe they are communicating with grandma or Aunt Nellie or dead rock stars, but I don't. In many cases what comes through in the guise of the human is actually inhuman, an entity that has waited for an opportunity to attack.

"You see, if someone we once knew and loved and

liked is going to come through, they will reach us on a level
that is easiest for them. That would be at the dream level,
or they would come through as a *visitation apparition,* or
as a *crisis apparition.* Typically they appear once or twice
and never ever again."

"Is this common?"

"Yes. And note people actually see the spirits. These
good spirits, often in solid form, standing at the foot of the
bed. I believe, and many of the clergy I've interviewed
believe, that these apparitions are a gift from God. However,
unlike bad spirits, these apparitions don't hang around. They
appear, communicate and go.

"We do have negative earthbound spirits, too. We have
homes that are haunted by spirits who have not accepted
their deaths and passed on. These are very confused spirits.
They are not aware that they have died, and they do not
come through the Ouija board! The proper response to
confused earthbound spirits is to tell them that they are
indeed dead and that they should go on. As we're talking,
Stoker; just as you and I are talking. Nothing weird, nothing
bizarre, nothing terrifying or frightening about it. Just talk
to them on a level that they can understand.

"But with the Ouija board, you're dealing with a
different phenomenon. You are conjuring spirits. And nonhuman spirits of a malicious nature tend to respond, not
human spirits. Human spirits are not waiting around for an
opportunity to come through on a Ouija board even though
you are trying to plug into them. They have no need to.
Whereas the entities attracted to the board are clumsy and
angry and confused and dangerous.

"I've been a psychic for many years, and I have used
my psychic abilities in many ways. I've discerned cases of
possession for the clergy. I've discerned for the police on
all levels of police work from federal down to civil, local
authorities. So I'm well aware of psychic ability because I

experience it firsthand. But I would never pick up a Ouija board! Under no circumstances whatsoever!"

"But Lorraine . . ."

"Many people claim to have psychic ability. Well, all of us have it to some degree or another. But why get involved with the Ouija board? Why not just use your psychic ability to discern whatever you wish to communicate with? The psychics who encourage people to fool around with the Ouija board are those who get others, particularly vulnerable young people, into trouble.

"We are often contacted by families, beautiful families, secure families, who purchased Ouija boards for their children as presents. Maybe the children use it right away; maybe they take it out of the closet five or six years later for a pajama party. The children are reaching the age of puberty; there are some frustrations, some hostilities that are being greatly repressed. Out comes the Ouija board and things start to happen. Why? Why are things suddenly happening? The answer is, Because the conditions are right."

"I see. So puberty is a time of greater possible psychic danger?"

"Yes, it is. Sexual changes are taking place, glandular changes. The same goes many times for middle-aged men and women. Both puberty and middle age are often periods of sexual frustration. Some people are able to vent this. Other interests in their lives take over; other means of expression become manifest. But some people don't vent."

"Developmental blockage?"

"Yes, exactly. When this energy buildup takes place, that person's aura changes. Spirits, you see, are attracted to our auras. They are attracted to the supernatural glow that surrounds us. And the type of person we are is what we attract. A person with an unhealthy aura attracts unhealthy spirits."

"Well, let me ask you this: as I'm working on

this book, am I drawing a lot of spirit attention to myself?"

"Yes, you are."

"All right. What do I do about that? How do I protect myself?"

"Are you a Catholic?"

"No, I was educated by nuns and priests, but I am not a Catholic."

"You will be!" Ed expostulated, and Lorraine quickly echoed, "You will be!"

"Very fast. You'll need your faith. We've never met anybody who was exposed to the diabolical whose faith wasn't made stronger. We're not saying Catholicism is the one true religion. But if you're Catholic, try to stick to your faith. Or if you're Protestant, try to stick with that faith."

"I have philosophical difficulties with organized religion."

"Forget about difficulties! If you continue with this work, you will need your religious faith to see you through safely. You must take spiritual precautions while researching and writing your book."

"What kind of precautions?"

"For one thing, be in a state of grace. If you can. You should envision yourself in a Christ light. A white light. A bright, white light that surrounds your physical body, your typewriter, the room that you are working in and your thoughts. You should do this every solitary time you sit down to work, and especially after nine o'clock at night. You know the worst phenomena occur between nine at night and six in the morning. These are the psychic hours."

Lorraine continued, "You probably have a little office. I suggest you get a small crucifix—it doesn't have to be a big one—and hang it over your work area. But first have it blessed by a very pious priest, not just any priest. And then, Stoker, during periods of time when you feel open, vulnerable, or weak or susceptible—or find your thoughts going astray—

look up to that crucifix as your source of strength. Don't fail to call on it. Never take it for granted."

"And if you ever experience what you would consider unnatural," Ed added, "say in a loud and clear voice, a commanding voice in the direction from which the sound is coming, or whatever it is you might be experiencing, 'In the name of Christ I command you to leave and go back to where you came from!' And make the sign of the cross in that direction. And I always suggest that you keep a powerful flashlight next to your bed at night."

"Why?"

"Spirits find it very hard to manifest in God's light, and many times in artificial light as well. If something should frighten you, if some biluminous form appears and you hit it with a powerful beam of light, it should disappear."

"This nine-to-six business. Is there any particular time of the year . . . ?"

"I'll tell you," Ed responded, "It's usually during the Lenten season, the holy season, that most of the diabolical possessions and infestations coming from the Ouija board take place. It's like an insult to Christianity itself."

"Now, while writing the book, I have a Ouija board in my house. Should I get rid of it?"

Ed and Lorraine answered quickly.

"Definitely!"

"Take it out of the house!"

"Bury it!"

"In about a foot and a half of earth! Cover it over!"

"Sprinkle it with holy water!"

"Make the sign of the cross!"

"Then leave it there!"

"But the ground is frozen hard now."

"Then go where there's a landfill taking place."

"Or bury it in a beachy area."

"What about burning it?"

"No!"

"No, don't burn it! People have taken Ouija boards, poured gasoline over them, and they wouldn't burn; then when they did burst into flame, the *people* felt as though they were burning! We've had cases like that."

"Oh. I appreciate your sincerity."

"It's our pleasure, Stoker."

"If you have any problems, just let us know."

"Thank you."

9

OUIJA OBSESSION
AND SPIRIT POSSESSION

In the last chapter we learned that Ed and Lorraine Warren believe the dead do not communicate through the Ouija board, that the spirits who do communicate via the Ouija are nonhumans masquerading as human, usually for mischievous, vicious or destructive reasons. But the vast majority of psychics and spiritualists disagree with the Warrens' interpretation. Their more widely held opinion is that many different kinds of beings communicate via the Ouija.

These include the human living, the human dead, nonhuman entities, and living and deceased animals. More often than not, the human dead are the most frequent communicators. Furthermore, the human dead who communicate via the Ouija board are often (perhaps most often) extremely confused spirits who, for a variety of reasons, cannot move on to the higher levels of afterlife. These are called the earthbound spirits. And in their confusion, anger, frustration and resistance, these earthbound intelligences can be dangerous: misleading, vengeful, corrupting and murderous. Given the opportunity, maladjusted earthbound entities attack the living. They assault, obsess and possess.

In the assault detailed earlier in this book, the victim was raped and brutalized by an entity that seemingly existed outside of and apart from the victim herself. In cases of obsession, the victim is forced to concern himself totally with the will of the vagrant spirit; once it dominates, this entity then schemes to get the victim to debase, deform, or—through suicide—destroy himself.

Sigmund Freud, the "father of psychoanalysis," established that many cases of mental illness exhibited some or all of the symptoms of historical or classic spirit possession. He coined the word *obsession,* now preferred because it lifted the consideration and treatment of these cases out of the realm of religion and the supernatural.

Strict religionists believe that of the three forms of spirit attack, possession is by far the most serious and terrifying. In possession cases, the hostile entity actually invades the body of the victim and uses, abuses, that body in any way it chooses. In possession cases, the victim becomes a human puppet whose strings are pulled by an irresistible, sadistic puppet master. And, to add to the horror, the victim is left fully aware of his fate. Consciously trapped in his own body, the victim can do nothing to save himself as his being is put through its diabolical paces.

Case Histories: Spirit Obsessions

Sally is not her real name. You've probably heard her records, perhaps called for encores at one of her performances. Her name is a household word, and she had a Ouija board experience that almost killed her.

It began innocently enough, as such cases always do. At first the messages Sally received through the board were amusing—gossip about her friends: their lives, what they were doing, what they were thinking about.

The messages proved accurate. Fascinated, Sally began consulting the Ouija board with greater frequency. Then the nightmare began—for Sally, her family and friends.

The apparently friendly voices began advising the star. Before it became apparent that the advice was not always in her best interests, it was too late. Sally had become addicted to the communications, and despite warnings from concerned loved ones, Sally followed the ghostly advice given her.

The Ouija voices assumed the guises of various religious leaders of great stature and led the star down a pathway of destruction. Despite a serious medical condition, Sally was told by the board to stop taking her necessary medication. Although terribly afraid of heights, Sally was persuaded to climb a dizzyingly steep nearby cliff. Soon she was coaxed to "Come to our side!" In an attempt to comply, Sally attempted suicide.

Sally is alive today, but the scars of her obsession experience will stay with her forever, both physically and psychologically.

Another victim is a single working woman who lived alone in Dallas. Miss B. had no close friends and was considered a loner.

When she discovered that the Ouija board would willingly communicate with her for hours on end, she was delighted, thrilled to have at last found an amusing, sincere, attentive "friend."

In due time, this unseen friend sent Miss B. to a local nightspot, the scene of the motion picture *Urban Cowboy*. It promised her she would meet the man of her dreams there. Miss B. uncritically followed the Ouija board's instructions. The result? She met the man of her nightmares; he beat her and brutally raped her. Now Miss B. spends her life in and out of hospitals and therapists' offices.

Because of the intimate nature of the information revealed, the Ouija board is incredibly seductive. The more suggestible a "player," the more dangerous the Ouija game. In early stages of obsession or possession, the victim becomes increasingly reliant on the Ouija board. He craves more and more revelations.

Soon the messages become the experimenter's sole interest. Normal activities and relationships become less important and even boring. The victim feels alert and alive only when working with the Ouija board.

Squandering vital nervous energy (vital if one is to get results from the Ouija), the drained victim—apathetic, lethargic, exhausted—is well on the way to disaster. Self-control and the ability to criticize fade. And the obsessed is easy prey to a spirit invader.

Case Histories: Possession

A case of possession is reported by Alan Vaughan in "Phantoms Stalked the Room . . ."—an autobiographical warning published in Martin Ebon's *The Satan Trap.* Vaughan's personal horror story began in 1965 when he was a college textbook editor specializing in chemistry and physics. At that time he was thoroughly skeptical about all things having to do with psychism or the occult, and he never considered the Ouija board to be connected to the "world of the real."

Out of simple curiosity he began to experiment with the Ouija board. He became hooked on the board when he and a friend contacted a spirit that, according to Vaughan, accurately predicted New York's 1973 flood, the worst in that city's history. The Ouija also revealed the then little-known fact that gossip columnist Dorothy Kilgallen had died, not naturally, but of barbiturate and alcoholic poisoning.

Fascinated, he and his Ouija became constant companions—at home and at work. He was hopelessly addicted to the board by the time that he received the first message from a spirit who called itself "Nada." "You are living, I am a spirit," Nada endlessly repeated. It seemed as though she might say nothing else. In time, and with great reluctance,

Nada did tell a little about herself: she had lived on Nantucket Island, had a daughter named Caxton and a husband who had died in 1912. Nada died in 1919. Although Vaughan found out little of her past life, it was clear that Nada was jealously obsessed with the idea that she was disembodied and Vaughan was not—a clear danger signal that the science editor failed to recognize or consider. Vaughan started to introduce Nada to all his personal and business friends, dragging the board with him from one end of Manhattan to the other, day and night.

When he couldn't find a certain friend one day, Nada volunteered to guide him. It was then, as the writer relates in horror, "I did the stupidest thing in my life." He invited Nada *into his body.*

Suddenly Nada was in control. And Vaughan was not. His body became the plaything of the neurotic entity Nada.

She jerked Vaughan out of his apartment and into the streets. Walking him quickly in one direction, then another, then another, Nada spun the terrified writer around in sudden about-faces again and again. She took him into buildings he did not know, building after building. Then, reeling, she returned him to the streets and the dark of night.

We don't know what happened next. Unfortunately, Vaughan reports no further.

Other Warnings

Here are the precious few examples of other people's awareness of the dangers of the Ouija I have been able to find.

In 1924, Dr. Carl Wickland wrote in his book, *Thirty Years Among the Dead,* "The serious problem of alienation and mental derangement attending ignorant psychic experiments was first brought to my attention by cases of several persons whose seemingly harmless experiences with automatic writing and the Ouija board resulted in such wild insanity that commitment to asylums was necessitated. . . . Many other disastrous results which followed the use of the supposedly innocent Ouija board came to my notice and my observations led me into research in psychic phenomena for a possible explanation of these strange occurrences."

In 1971, a painfully personal book, *Confessions of a Psychic,* was written by Susy Smith. She wrote, "Warn people away from Ouija and automatic writing until you have learned how to be fully protected. They say that innocent efforts at communication are as dangerous as playing with matches or hand grenades. They have me as Exhibit A of what not to do, for I experienced many of the worst problems of such involvement. Had I been forewarned by my reading that such efforts might cause one to run the risk of being mentally disturbed, I might have been more wary."

And in 1972, Robert H. Ashby wrote in *The Guide Book for the Study of Psychical Research,* "Many researchers have pointed out the inherent dangers of using the Ouija board or of taking its messages seriously, because of the possibility of dredging up some very unpleasant and potentially disturbing attitudes and facts from one's subconscious. There have been numerous instances of persons who have become very upset emotionally from the use of the Ouija board."

In 1964, Hugh Lynn Cayce, the son of the "Seer of Virginia Beach," Edgar Cayce, published a book, *Venture Inward.* In a damning chapter, "Automatic Writing and Ouija Boards," the psychic researcher wrote of the difficulties some people face in exploring the unconscious. "They are not uncommon, unfortunately. The frightening thing about them is that they can be duplicated by the thousands from the case histories of present-day inmates of mental institutions all over the world."

One story from his files deals with a young mother

who worked the Ouija board originally with her husband. The board told her she was a "sensitive"; it told her where she could find lost objects, warned her of accidents with her children, gave her information about the thoughts and actions of her neighbors (which greatly astonished them with their accuracy and details) and also convinced her to do automatic writing. One morning the woman heard a voice behind her left ear. At first it was a soft voice, telling her helpful things. But in a matter of days the voice turned harsh and ugly. He identified himself as a discarnate spirit in love with her. He told her he was going to kill her so they could be together on the "same plane." From that point on she could eat no food without great effort; even when she tried just to drink a little water he would appear to her suddenly and force her to vomit. One day, when her husband had left for work early, the woman was horrified to realize she was not alone in bed. The spirit was with her. Despite her protests and abject terror, it sexually assaulted her. Before this, the woman had rejected going for professional help, afraid she would be permanently institutionalized. She no longer had this fear. She ran to her daughters' room (the spirit seemed to weaken when she was with her daughters), called her husband and had him take her to a psychiatrist. Eventually, through psychiatric treatment that included prayer, physiotherapy and the help of a psychically gifted person, she was enabled to return to a nearly normal life.

The Traditional Pathology of the Spirit Attack

It may be difficult for most of us to accept the notion of evil spirits that take a fancy to our bodies and minds. It may seem too much like the theme of many late-night class-B horror movies or cheap science fiction paperbacks. But there is no doubt about the reality of invading spirits in the minds of those I interviewed or in the material I read in preparing this book.

Those most concerned about these things believe that we are protected from these entities by a halo of light and color—an energy field that surrounds the bodies of all living things—an aura that can be discerned by many psychics and recorded by Kirlian photography. They say that the aura and the life of an individual are inseparable—and that changes in its color and shape are parallel responses to an individual's changing health, character, mood, even spiritual nature. They believe that once the protective emanation— the aura—is split or entangled, the invading entity can undermine its would-be victim and create a sense of dependency within him. That is the strategy.

But tactics vary. The attack can be brutal and sudden: spiritual blitzkrieg. But that is seldom the case. More typically it's a matter of gradual seduction. Even brutal attack usually occurs only after a subtle campaign of masquerade and seduction has weakened the victim.

The invader focuses on the victim's character weaknesses. These weaknesses, of course, vary from victim to victim. If one is vain, appeals to vanity are made. "I need help," the seducer will say, "and only you can help me." Sometimes a victim is told that he is meant to accomplish a great work of some kind, and that working together (victim and entity), the work can be accomplished. This is a common tactic.

As far as the invading entity is concerned, *any* emotional response by the victim is desirable, even a negative response. The appeals vary, but the intention is always the same: to establish a relationship and nurture a dependency. The entity is malicious and does not hesitate to lie, misrepresent itself (usually as a deceased loved one) and flatter.

If it better serves the entity's purposes, it will switch tactics and try to exhaust its victim, try to arouse fear—

anything to maintain the relationship, anything to hold the victim's attention once it has been caught.

It's better for the invader, of course, if the victim is alone, isolated, exhausted and ill. Thus, the entity will encourage its victim to drop real friends and rely only on Ouija communications for counsel, advice and companionship. To this end, it will send the victim on wild, purposeless trips. It will recommend dangerous stunts and wild adventures while discouraging healthy activities and proper medical care.

If need be, the invader will terrify its victim, material-izing in ghastly form, inducing grotesque visions, inciting poltergeist activity, causing objects to appear out of the blue (apports), delivering false or tragic news, levitating objects, perhaps levitating the victim. All of these things and more might be done—not as ends in themselves but as means to an eventual complete possession. If fear will allow the invader to overwhelm the victim, then fear it will be. The strategy is to make the victim believe that opposition to the invader is useless. When the victim finally believes that resistance is futile, the possession is completed.

Negative Earthbound Enemies

It is believed that the earthbound spirits are, most frequently, those who led troubled, destructive lives on earth. When one is graduated from life to death, there is no profound change in basic character. Those who led vicious, violent lives while on earth will also be vicious and violent after death. It is this negativity that prevents most earthbound spirits from understanding or accepting that they are indeed dead. They linger because earthly appetites continue to overwhelm them. They are frustrated and angry because they cannot satisfy those appetites. The earth tyrant, social or domestic, is also a tyrant in the afterlife plane; a will to dominate and control others will continue to drive this personality even after death. These are the people you avoid in your ordinary daily life; Ouija experimentation invites them into your life. And once invited, they will jump at the chance to be with you, to be part of you, to *be* you!

Sociologist and author Ian Currie explained the earth-bound dead this way. A serious misconception about death is that, since death turns persons into spirits, the spirits automatically become spiritual—benevolent, wise, all-know-ing. This assumption about the dead could scarcely be more wrong. The borderline between the worlds of the living and of the dead appears to be a sort of "ineffectively policed psychic jungle, an outlaw territory thronged with vicious psychopathic entities." If these deranged entities locate and attune themselves to a living victim, the violent and destruc-tive natures of these earthbound dead will operate with even *less restraint* than in the flesh.

Accidental Obsession or Possession

So obsession can occur when an earthbound spirit wants to take control and deliberately chooses to enter a living person. But all obsession or possession is not the result of such deliberation. It can happen accidentally. This, it is believed by many, occurs when, through a Ouija experience, an earthbound spirit becomes entangled in the aura of the Ouija operator without intending to and without knowing how to disentangle itself.

This accidental relationship can be mild or vicious, depending on the personality of the earthbound. The obses-sion can be brief and relatively painless if all the earthbound has to do is say good-bye to someone before moving on to the proper sphere. However, the earthbound could have a violent, destructive nature; and it might have no intention of ever seeking its proper sphere. This is the relationship that can cause the victim a catalog of agony.

Ouija experimentation apparently heightens the operator's aura in certain attention-getting ways, altering the intensity, shape, and/or coloring of the aura. Confused earthbound spirits or nonhuman entities existing in the misty darkness are attracted to the heightened glow of the aura. It seems a refuge, an oasis of light in a world of darkness. When the curious entity approaches the light to investigate, be it deliberate or through some form of magnetism or clumsiness, the entanglement occurs.

The entity now has no choice but to accompany the living person. The entity becomes even more confused, and can come to think of the person as a jailer, or an ever-present and annoying "body" guard.

Even worse, regardless of whether the entanglement was accidental or deliberate, it may evolve into a full possession, the actual occupation of the living person's body. Trapped in that body, the entity begins to think of the body as its own. In time, it tries to drive the original human intelligence out of the living body.

An Exorcism

William Peter Blatty based his best-selling novel and screenplay *The Exorcist* on an actual case of possession and exorcism that took place in 1949. In Blatty's fictionalization, it was a teenage girl who was invaded by a demon after the girl's aunt and mother had experimented with a Ouija board. The actual victim was a 14-year-old boy named Douglas Deen.

The story was first reported in the Washington *Post,* on August 20, 1949. The headline read, "Priest Frees Mt. Rainier [Md.] Boy Reported Held in Devil's Grip." It's first line is, "In what is perhaps one of the most remarkable experiences of its kind in recent religious history, a 14-year-old Mount Rainier boy has been freed by a Catholic priest

of possession by the devil, Catholic sources reported
yesterday."

J. B. Rhine, director of the parapsychological laboratory
at Duke University, investigated the case and was quoted
as saying it was "the most impressive" poltergeist phenomenon he had ever come across.

The word *poltergeist* comes from the Greek word
meaning "noise ghost." Some of the manifestations included:

• the bed in which the boy was sleeping moving across
the room
• a heavy armchair tilting and falling over, spilling the
boy who was sitting in it, his chin resting on his knees
• in the boy's presence, fruit placed on the refrigerator
jumping up and hurling itself against a wall
• scratching noises from the walls near where the boy
stood

Neighbors of the Deens first laughed off the phenomena
and said their house was known to be haunted. But when
Douglas visited their houses, the manifestations continued,
including violent, apparently involuntary shakings of the
boy's bed.

The Deens turned to their minister for help. Originally
skeptical, he invited Douglas to his house. The minister was
convinced when he witnessed several manifestations, including the one in which the heavy armchair tipped over. He
then tried to tip the chair over while sitting in it, but he
couldn't.

A 50-year-old Jesuit priest from Saint Louis then
observed the boy and the manifestations. For two months
he stayed with him; sometimes even slept in the same room.
He took the boy to Georgetown University Hospital for
extensive studies, and to Saint Louis University Hospital.
Exorcism was agreed upon only after all other possible cures
had been exhausted.

The boy's parents were not Catholic, so before the

exorcism the boy had to convert and receive religious instruction.

Twenty to thirty performances of the ritual were held, each lasting about three quarters of an hour. The priest, having fasted, started by saying Mass and praying for divine strength. More prayers and psalms followed. He then sprinkled holy water on the boy and read the twenty-seven-page ritual, which ordered the evil spirit to depart.

> "I command you, whoever you are, unclean spirit, and all of your associates, obsessing this friend of God, that by the mysteries of the Incarnation, Passion, Resurrection and Ascension of our Lord Jesus Christ, by the mission of the Holy Spirit and by the coming of the same Master for the Judgment, give me your name, the day and hour of your exit, together with some sign, and even though I am an unworthy minister of God, I command thee to obey in all these things nor ever again in any matter to offend this creature of God, or, those who are here or any of their possessions. . . .
>
> "Depart therefore, in the name of the Father, the Son and the Holy Ghost, give place to the Holy Spirit through this sign of the Holy Cross of Jesus Christ our Lord who with the Father and the same Holy Spirit lives and reigns now and forever, Amen."

The boy at first reacted violently to this—screaming, cursing, and talking in Latin, a language he had never studied. At one point he claimed he had a vision of Saint Michael casting out the devil.

Finally the priest announced the boy was cured. The manifestations had stopped.

The Washington *Post* reported that exorcisms and cases of diabolical possession are very rare in the western Christian world. The solemn rite of exorcism was quite possibly the first performed in the Washington area. Permission to hold the exorcism must be received from the archbishop after full documentation and verification.

Automatistic View of Spirit Possession

Naturally those who reject the idea that real spirits communicate through the Ouija also reject the idea of Ouija possession. Katharine Cover Sabin, a noted psychic and parapsychological researcher, claims she has witnessed twenty-two cases of possession—but found none of them convincing.

Both Ouija and automatic writing are "ESP methods that can endanger the mind," she says. They are "unnatural physiological and mental processes during which the volition of the hands is surrendered to exteriorized energy while the subconscious spells or writes out messages." This is particularly dangerous because exteriorized energy can also administer "pinches, blows, sexual orgasm, and even disturbances in the environment."

One reason why Katharine Cover Sabin doubts the existence of spirit possession is because all such cases, she says, can be treated by psychiatrists. The patients are diagnosed as having "mental dissociation"; they are first tranquilized, then brought into greater social contact with others, then the psychiatrist will try to convince them that there are no evil spirits—they have simply been the victims of repression and their own exteriorized energy.

10

RELIGIONS VERSUS THE OUIJA

Fundamentalist View

Most of the religions of the western world oppose the use of the Ouija, although the Fundamentalist religions are far more passionate and vehement in their opposition. This is because the Fundamentalists firmly believe the Ouija is an instrument of the Devil. Satan, they say, works through the Ouija board, uses it to ensnare and seduce innocent victims, thereby attacking God through the abuse of His creation.

Pastor A. N. How, the secretary of the Canadian Union Conference of the Seventh Day Adventist, declares, "The Ouija board is extremely dangerous, pure and simple. I would not under any conditions have such a frightful thing in my home!"

There are, according to the Fundamentalist Christian view of reality, real and present dangers associated with its use. They insist that those who work with the Ouija board are knowingly or unknowingly placing themselves in extreme spiritual and physical danger.

The Reverend Stuart Mulligan of the Pentecostal church firmly made this point when he testified, without hesitation, "The board should not be permitted under any circumstances in a Christian home. The use of the Ouija board and the faithful practice of Christianity is a serious contradiction. It is strongly forbidden, extremely dangerous."

The New Testament contains close to one hundred references to demons and evil spirits. At least seven types of nonmaterial beings, some more wicked than others, all of them unclean in the eyes of God, are identified: "spirits" (*Mt* 8:16), "foul spirits" (*Mk* 9:25), "evil spirits" (*Lk* 7:21), "deaf and dumb spirits" (*Mk* 9:25), "spirits of infirmity" (*Lk* 13:11), "spirits of divination" (*Ac* 16:16), and "deceitful spirits" (*I Ti* 4:1–2). These spirits are not mere metaphors for the Fundamentalist Christian. They are literal facts. With unblinking faith the literalist Christian insists that intelligent spiritual beings clearly identified as devils or demons do exist to torture and destroy us.

Traditionally, these demons are fallen angels, those who joined Satan to oppose the will of God. The traditional Christian view holds that demons are of two categories: confined and unconfined. The confined stay forever in hell; the unconfined are Satan's emissaries and are free to wander where they will, or go where Satan orders them. These demons, great in number ("My name is Legion, for we are many" [*Mk* 5:9]), are viewed as personal beings, each with personality, intelligence, sensibility and will. They think, speak and act. They are alive and loose among us, working their wills, entering and possessing human victims to defy, antagonize and demean God.

"Are we justified in talking about the demonic? Most definitely! People are today recognizing more and more that the demonic is by no means just some outdated Biblical concept," wrote Dr. Alfred Lechler, a Christian psychiatrist. He believes that demonic assault and possession "is a terrible reality which one must increasingly reckon with today."

The reality of evil embodied as living, vital forces active and hostile among us is the principal subject matter of continual Fundamentalist concern.

The real need for exorcism—the driving out of evil spirits in the name of Christ—is summarized by J. Stafford Wright in his book *Christianity and the Occult*. He wrote, "The tendency today is to regard all the phenomena as of psychological origin. Yet Jesus believed in [demonic possession] and distinguished between normal illnesses to be cured by laying-on of hands or anointing, and demon possession to be cured by word of command. Any practicing psychologist who would cure an extensive complex of compulsive phenomena—as such possession has been called—by word of command would soon . . . clear up the waiting lists that are a nightmare of psychiatry."

The Fundamentalist view of the Ouija board and the demonic powers they associate with the Ouija board is completely and aggressively negative. For the Fundamentalist, there is no doubt about it. The Ouija board is—without question, without qualification—a most dangerous game!

The Ouija board, however, seems to be minimally tolerated by non-Fundamentalist Christian religions. Ouijaing seems to be acceptable if kept trivialized, but condemned if internalized. The difference between the condemnation of the Fundamentalist and the non-Fundamentalist religions seems to be one of degree, of emphasis, not of essential principle. Father Alex Gerard of the National (Canadian) Catholic Information Center lays his traditional, condemnatory explanation of official Catholic policy right on the hard line: "If the Ouija is approached seriously, if one actually turns to it for advice or comfort, it is definitely sinful. It is a flagrant insult to the real dignity of both God and man, a clear abuse of the First and Second Commandments!"

Arleon L. Kelley, Th.D., assistant general secretary of the National Council of Churches, writes, "It is my personal opinion that those in the mainline churches would understand the Ouija board and similar phenomena to be in the realm of the parapsychological. They would not see it as an evil force unless it came to the place that more faith were given to the Ouija board than to God." Dr. Kelley also said, "Most thinking church people would be the first to admit that there are many phenomena in the creation which we as yet have not come to fully understand. But because we do not understand them does not mean that we should trust them or distrust them. I believe an authentic Christian is one who is open to the continuing revelation of God and to the mysteries of creation."

Mother Anne Garrison, an Episcopal priest, says, "A lot of these rather beguiling pursuits tend to divert our attention. I believe Saint Paul would have found the Ouija board frivolous and ultimately time-wasting. I think there are far more important things to do as religiously directed people. We need to remember where our attention as religiously obedient people ought to be.

"The Old Testament came down very hard on anything that smacked of necromancy. I wouldn't say that playing around with the Ouija board is necessarily morally destructive. I would simply say that it is to Satanism what putting nickels in a slot machine is to roulette."

Even some people who wholeheartedly believe that the Ouija is an automatism fear that the experimenter too often keys into a lowered sense of morality that has been suppressed in his subconscious. The fear is that people will accept decisions or perform acts that they would not do, because they can shift responsibilities from themselves on to the board.

Judaism and Ouija Psychism

God's purpose in regard to humankind, according to the traditional or Orthodox Judaic view, is to heighten and charge man's existence with freedom. The primary moral directive is to live in the present, not the past or future. Jews are directed to exercise free will, always to choose to live a moral life despite humankind's innate animality. The ethical ideal is right behavior at all times.

Sin as such, as well as a belief in Satan or hell, is more important in Christian eschatology than in Jewish. The Hebrew scripture is not concerned with Satan, Beelzebub or fallen angels. Revelations about spirits, spirit communication and spirit divination are found in the Torah. Deuteronomy 18:10 discusses divination through "charmed" natural instruments which might be likened to the Ouija board. Historical Jewish sages knew how easily one could fall to misuse of the paranormal, and specifically to the overuse of a spirit guide. "At first he becomes a guest; afterward, he becomes the master," says Midrash Bereishin Rabbah.

Necromancy—direct conversation with a spirit of the human dead—interferes with a full, sincere relationship with the living God. The practicing Jew therefore refrains from psychism of this kind. Some paranormal activities, however, are allowable by Judaic standards. These include astrology, astral projection, linguistic numerology and non-spiritual demonology (the golem, for example). Historically, all paranormal activities were kept deliberately esoteric, actively hidden from the masses. Discussions about these matters are expounded only in the Kabbala ("The Tradition"), a body of literature meant only for the eyes of highly trained and especially holy initiates. While there is no mention of the Ouija board in the Kabbala, there are numerous mentions of automatic writing and even table levitation.

Isaac Mozeson, a poet whose primary interest as an artist is addressing the Jewish people, is also a linguist who has translated Genesis. Educated at Yeshiva University, Mozeson believes that he is one of the few American Jews who make a study of the paranormal.

"The Torah cannot and will not deny or rationalize away the true phenomenon of spirit communication through various forms, including the Ouija board," he says. Mozeson emphasizes that the Torah takes for granted the "literal existence and long-standing practice of communicating with the dead—and forbids Jews this practice. King Saul, for example, was denigrated for communicating with the deceased prophet Samuel through a medium."

The use of the Ouija board, then, to communicate with the dead is a serious negative matter, an act that taints one and damages one's relationship with the living God. Leviticus 20:27, as translated by Isaac Mozeson, says, "A man or woman who communes with the departed or with a spirit guide ought to forfeit their own physical lives. . . ." But Mozeson points out, "Punishments for capital crimes were almost never carried out. Such crimes and their punishments are on the books primarily as deterrents."

According to Mozeson, Orthodox Judaism acknowledges the reality of Ouija board phenomena and clearly warns against its psychospiritual hazards. "Only the exceptional sage should delve into these awesome sciences," Mozeson concludes, "and then only for the *greater good of the community*. . . ."

Witchcraft and the Ouija Board

The most maligned (and possibly most ancient) of the western religions is witchcraft, also known as Wicca, or The Craft. Over the centuries, practitioners of witchcraft have been suppressed, even subjected to genocidal attacks.

Yvonne and Gavin Frost are the founders of the Church and School of Wicca headquartered in New Bern, North Carolina. The material that follows is based on an exclusive interview, for this book, with Yvonne Frost.

"The basic principles of The Craft are five in number. *One, the Wiccan Rede.* 'Harm none, do what you will.' As long as you're not going to harm anybody, including yourself, do what you like and don't bother with guilt.

Two, reincarnation. Reincarnations are like semesters in school, always advancing. When we are finished with the human experience, we go on to higher levels. At this earth level, we are far from complete, far from perfect.

Three, power through knowledge. Through knowledge we can learn to manipulate the cosmic energy that rains upon the earth and supplement the energy in our bodies.

Four, the law of attraction. What you are is what you will draw to yourself. If you are kind and helpful to other living creatures, you'll get back helpful, kind, compassionate experiences. If you act with hate and vicious intent, you will attract vicious, hateful experiences.

Five, harmony. There is a harmonious pattern to the world, and we can see it in the waxing and waning of the moon, the rising and setting of the sun, and the cycles of the seasons.

Wicca believes that in addition to the deity and the human, other intelligences—evolving and higher than human—also exist. These evolving entities ("Elder Ones") can be positive or negative in character.

Yvonne strongly suggests the Ouija board be avoided, insisting that it is foolish to encourage communication with the negative entities. As for communicating with the positive entities, she says it is much better done by other means. She recommends meditative sessions instead.

"Operating the Ouija board is like opening the door to your spiritual dwelling and leaving it open," she says. "The Elder Ones might then enter, and you can't tell which one might come along. Without taking precautions of exactly the right kind, you are making yourself vulnerable to many unpredictable experiences."

Rapping, Clapping and Spiritualism

The only "religion" that approves of the Ouija board is Spiritualism. Spiritualism isn't a true religion, despite its interest in the metaphysical, because it never developed a body of theological dogma. Still, the fervency of its adherents and the claims made on its behalf certainly make it seem like a religious movement.

Spiritualism pure and simple is a belief in spirits, "that the dead can and do communicate with the living," as the dictionary puts it. But the movement as it is now understood began in Hydesville, New York, in 1848 with what appeared to be a Ouija-like phenomenon. There, in a shanty, lived two Methodist sisters, Margaret (aged 15) and Kate (12) Fox. Their home had a reputation in the neighborhood as being the seat of odd occurrences even before the sisters had moved into it with their parents. There were mysterious knocks, rappings and bangs. The sisters, frightened, insisted on sleeping with their worried mother and father.

The girls discovered that they could communicate with the "spirit" haunting their humble home. They did this by clapping their hands. Each time they did so, the spirit replied with a clapping sound, a perfect echo.

Through this communication, a haunting story emerged. A man had been murdered in the house and it was this man with whom the Fox sisters were communicating. He told them that he had been murdered by a traveling peddler and that his corpse was then buried in the basement of the house. Fifty-six years later, in 1904, a complete male skeleton was found buried in the shanty's basement.

When a married sister returned home for a visit and discovered the amazing things going on, she organized a "Society of Spiritualists," and allowed the local populace to see the children. Hydesville became famous overnight. News of the rappings spread not only throughout the United States, but also across Europe.

The clamor to see Margaret and Kate became overwhelming. The young children put on public exhibitions that drew giant crowds in Rochester, and then in New York City. From there they launched a tour of the United States, which attracted the "most prominent theologians, physicians, and professional men of all kinds, as well as great crowds everywhere."

When the grand tour ended, Horace Greeley, the famed newspaper editor, sponsored Kate's education, while Margaret began a series of seances in Philadelphia. He also enthusiastically publicized the Spiritualist movement in his newspaper, the New York *Tribune.*

Spiritualism became a major international movement. In 1852 the first Spiritualist convention was held in Cleveland. Converts flocked by the tens of thousands. By the 1870's, there were an estimated eight million spiritualists in the United States alone. The Fox sisters became world-famous celebrities. Before too long, other seance mediums became almost equally famous. The mediumistic repertoire was typically expanded to include levitations, the production of ectoplasms, the movement of objects, trumpets, gloves, etc.

Something of a turning point was reached when Dr. Walter Franklin Prince, in his role of research officer for the American Society of Psychical Research, traveled to many countries and throughout the United States attending and investigating seances. He exposed several well-known mediums as outright frauds. In general, though, he simply and coolly reported the facts of the seances as he directly observed them, allowing the readers to draw their own conclusions. The Psychical Society determined to stop spending large amounts of money investigating seances. But Prince's reports didn't discourage an enthusiastic international public.

An even greater turning point occurred in 1888. Margaret Fox, whose married life was tragic and who had taken to drinking, wrote an article for the New York *World* detailing her history and saying she was a fraud. She said it was her "sacred duty" to expose Spiritualism.

At first, she wrote, she and her sister mischievously teased their mother by tying an apple to a string and moving the string up and down, which caused the apple to bump on the floor. Their mother, a very nervous, gullible and superstitious woman, worried that a disembodied spirit had taken possession of her children. This encouraged the children to learn new, more sophisticated means of trickery. They learned to make rapping noises with their fingers and toes.

The next thing Margaret knew, she and her sister were world-famous and fairly rich, traveling in high society and meeting fascinating people. In her article, Margaret said she had wanted to admit she was a fraud from the beginning, only she didn't dare to.

The day her article appeared in the paper, Margaret remained secluded in her hotel, fearful of being kidnapped by irate mediums. But that night she gave an exhibition to demonstrate her fraud at the Brooklyn Academy of Music. The overflow crowd witnessed Margaret "summon" the spirits of Abraham Lincoln and Napoleon. She asked the spirits questions, and they responded in ridiculous fashion. They seemed to rap their answers on the table Margaret had set next to her onstage—but a committee of doctors, also asked onstage to investigate, unanimously and immediately concluded that the noises had been produced by Margaret's big toe.

But Spiritualism was not dead by any means. Some people pooh-poohed Margaret's confession, saying she was a hopeless alcoholic and not responsible for her actions anymore. Some said she had been bribed. Indeed, Margaret later recanted her confession and tried again to earn money by giving seances. But her reputation had been shattered. She died penurious in 1895.

Houdini and the Spiritualists

One of the foremost spiritualist researchers was the great magician Houdini. Early in his career he held seances and "communicated with the spirits of the dead" for his clients.

At first he thought it merely a sideline to his professional work as a mystifier, but he came to regret his deceptions. He realized that the people who attended his seances did not want to be entertained, as did the audiences who attended his stage performances. They desperately wanted to contact their loved ones, and they took his sorcery seriously. They were vulnerable.

Houdini stopped giving seances, but he didn't stop attending them. When his mother died, he was distraught. It became his most fervent wish in life to speak with her again. (He felt sure she would be waiting for him at the gates of heaven when he died.) For thirty years he delved into Spiritualism, collecting a huge library on the subject and investigating every medium who claimed some kind of success.

No one was more hopeful of Spiritualism than Houdini—and no one more disappointed. Because of his expertise in the ways of magic, he knew all the tricks "mediums" could try. He knew how to set up test conditions that disallowed the mediums from using fraud. Suddenly all their spectacular successes were unreproducible. In all his years of inquiry, Houdini never met a genuine medium.

Eventually he became so disgusted and convinced of the fraud of Spiritualism that he spoke out against it—publishing the fakes he had unmasked in such books as *A Magician Among the Spirits*. In this book he quoted experts such as Dr. George M. Robertson, superintendent of the Royal Edinburgh Mental Hospital, who warned that, from his observation, the strong belief in Spiritualism by neurotics greatly increased their chance of insanity.

Houdini also quoted a Dr. Curry, medical director of the state insane asylum of New Jersey, who said of the Ouija board, "[It] is especially serious because it is adopted mainly by persons of high-strung neurotic tendency who become victims of actual illusions of sight, hearing and touch at Spiritualistic seances." Dr. Curry predicted that if the popularity of the Ouija board didn't die down, the insane asylums would be "flooded with patients." In another story from this book, Houdini reports that in March 1920, five people in Carrito, California, were driven mad by the Ouija board.

OUIJA

AND THE
PSYCHOLOGISTS

11

THE PHILIP EXPERIMENT

A lthough Faraday proved that table-rapping was a form of automatism and Houdini debunked every spirit medium he was able to study, the interest in mediums, ghosts and communicating with the spirit world still runs high. The age-old questions are still being pondered. Do ghosts exist? Do seances actually raise the spirits of the dead? If not, how can one explain the physical phenomena that seances sometimes generate? Can these phenomena be reproduced by ordinary people without the presence of a spirit medium?

These questions were raised by some of the members of the Toronto Society of Psychical Research, a nonprofit association founded in 1970 "to promote research on the frontiers of science and disseminate information." To search for answers to these questions, a dedicated group of society volunteers, a cross-section of ordinary citizens, none of them mediums, agreed to meet regularly in a fully lit room to see if they could produce seance-type effects—not by inviting spirits to communicate with them, but by projecting a previously agreed upon, concentrated group thought.

The idea was to see if they could manifest an imaginary character. They therefore deliberately concocted a totally fictitious biography for a nonexistent person. They named him Philip.

This is the "true" story of Philip. A Catholic English aristocrat of the 1600's, Philip was in the uncomfortable position of having supported the overthrown Catholic king, Charles I. Oliver Cromwell was then in power. Philip's frigid, vicious wife, Dorothea, often used Philip's unfortunate political standing as a weapon against him. She threatened to campaign politically against her husband, which could have easily lost him his reputation, his title and all his worldly possessions.

This marital situation was made even more dangerous when Philip foolishly fell in love with an Esmeralda-type Gypsy girl and even more foolishly installed her as his lover in the gatehouse of Diddington, Philip's ancestral home. When Dorothea discovered this unwelcome news, she publically accused the girl of witchcraft and had the supreme satisfaction of seeing her burned at the stake.

This filled Philip with despair. Finally, after long, horrible months of pacing the battlements of Diddington, Philip threw himself from the walls of his ancestral home.

This tragic but deliberately silly ghost is the personality the Toronto group of experiments set out to conjure. After each of the experimenters memorized the supposed biography (and there were a good many more details), they gathered faithfully together and meditated on schedule, waiting for results.

Nothing happened; however, the group continued to meet regularly as a strong group rapport formed.

Finally it was decided that a new approach would be attempted. They'd try a seance. After all, spirit raisings were often obtained through table-rapping. All the previously agreed-upon rules could be kept; meetings would continue to be held in brightly lit rooms; the group would continue to focus on the fictitious biography as already developed.

They held their first seance.

Someone responded. Knocks were heard in the table

beneath the experimenters' hands. One rap for Yes, two for No. It was Philip.

The conversation, once started, went on for five years. The manufactured ghost became extremely adept at producing a variety of knocks on request. He even developed the ability to transfer his responses to objects apart from the table around which the conjuring group sat. One such object was a suspended metal plate. When the knocks produced in the plate were tape-recorded, an electronic analysis clearly indicated that the Philip soundings were *distinctive,* unlike all other sounds on the tape.

The Philip experiment strongly supports the idea that both Philip, and the wide range of phenomena associated with Philip, are products of the group's collective conscious and subconscious knowledge. Why? Because Philip's responses *never* deviated from the logic determined by the fictitious biography. As the conversation went on, and as Philip expanded on his stories, the details he added and the further incidents he revealed were always logical extensions of the original group-invented story. The personality of Philip via his communications was made clearer, sharper, more distinct; but again, always only in terms of the assigned biography.

It's interesting to note that if the group deliberately made a change in the original biography, Philip inevitably accepted the change. And if the group did not know the answer to a specific question, Philip did not know that answer either. Nor, like the group, was Philip capable of predicting the future.

And what are the conclusions? Well, of course, the idea of spirits and spirit communication can never be entirely disproven; but this experiment certainly argues that if people want to believe in spirits hard enough, their wishes will come true.

Allen Spraggett looks at it this way. In the October 1974 issue of *Psychic* magazine, he wrote, "We have shown that a group of people can create a thought-directed force that can be expressed in a physical way."

Later, a second group was formed by the Toronto SPR to find out if the original experiment could be duplicated. In less than five weeks of focused effort, the second group was effectively communicating with *its* imaginary personality.

As of this writing, the Philip experiment has been duplicated dozens of times by groups all over the world.

"We clearly understand and have proved that there is no 'spirit' behind the communications," one group experimenter commented, "but it is the physical force that we need to know more about."

How do these materializations of fictitious characters work? Iris M. Owen and Margaret Sparrow investigated the processes and analyzed the results in their book *Conjuring Up Philip: An Adventure in Psychokinesis.*

Group rapport seems to be the primary matter—the sympathy and empathy that develops within the group as its individual members spend a great deal of focused time in each other's company. As emotional tension grows, it finds release in group telepathy. The authors also pondered the validity of these experiments.

"Our discoveries show that one can no longer say, as many people do, that the physical phenomena of the seance room are always fraudulent, because they may, for all we know to the contrary, be genuine PK effects. On the other hand, we cannot be sure that they are due to a spirit because they may be *merely* PK effects, and the 'communicator' allegedly present may be purely imaginary like Philip.

"Telepathy seems to take place, and to exist between ordinary people who make no claim to psychic ability, and even at times between people who seem to have no awareness that it is happening," write Iris Owen and Margaret Sparrow in their book. "If this is true, and experiments seem to show that it is, then the collective hallucination theory of ghost sightings seems tenable. Just as in a group situation one can produce telepathy, could it not happen that if a group of people had a mutual rapport they might see a ghost together as a group?"

A second, separate research paper relating to the Philip experiment was published in the June 1977 issue of *New Horizons*. It has to do with a pilot experiment conducted by Frank J. Riley as he tried to tape-record Philip. Fifteen experimental sessions each produced taped voices or voicelike sounds. These ranged from faint whispers of words and phrases to easily heard statements.

Some of the taped Philip responses are difficult to recognize. But others are easily and clearly heard when the tapes are played back.

On April 7, 1977, Frank Riley, the Philip group and their chairman, Dr. A. R. G. Owen, moved the tape-recording experiment into a special steel and concrete room in the University of Toronto. Riley describes the room as "quadruply shielded electromagnetically with power lines isolated and ballasts from the fluorescent lights externalized." The entire room is "suspended on springs to make it vibration proof."

Again, a number of voices were audible when the group's session tape was played back. In an extension of the experiment, the Philip group silently thought about a predetermined word kept secret from Riley for two minutes.

After the session, Frank Riley played the noted tape-recorded silence back. But where there should have been a silence, a voice was heard. But the voice was unclear. Riley listened to it, however, many times, and he finally made note of his interpretation of the voice's word(s). His identification: *Bernie's hat*. When Riley revealed this to the group, the group announced that its predetermined secret word was *bananas*. How did that sound get on the tape? No one knows.

As the years passed and the experiment continued, Philip was able to demonstrate more and more abilities.

Levitations occurred. "Pings" were induced in nearby objects made of tin and in metal sheets. Voice manifestations were successfully tape-recorded. Intergroup communications became commonplace. Additional personalities were contacted.

But the research is far from over. "We have not yet been able to ascertain how the raps occur in a physical sense; we have acquired more skill in controlling them, we can play tunes, count ahead, produce remote raps in metal and in the furniture around, but we still do not understand how it is done," Iris Owen wrote in *New Horizons.* "Nonetheless, the research committee and the Philip group believe that group psychokinesis and in particular the projection of controlled fantasy or drama has been and will continue to be an important research method which, it is hoped, will be taken up by others, doubtless with improvements. We also welcome suggestions for new research by ourselves on 'Philipian' lines."

I asked Iris how the Ouija board and table-rapping relate to each other. "Most Ouija board communications, like those in the Philip experiment, come from the subconscious minds of the operators or from those around them. Of course, that's a controversial idea, because there are those who believe that the communicators are the spirits of those who have passed over. However, our research and our experiments support our interpretation. The point is that when you understand how the mind works, you realize how the mind plays around. It's as if the mind were picking up all sorts of bricks all over the place and building a new building. Or picking up words and phrases and writing a new story. The principles that apply to the Philip experiment apply to the Ouija board.

"I have a personal example of this playful Ouija quality. During the Second World War, I was in the forces. Sitting around the barracks at night, we'd pull out the Ouija boards, and everybody's subconscious fears emerged. People were getting very upset, very disturbed because all sorts of strange messages were coming out. In wartime, everyone's subconscious fears emerge and frighten them, and one quickly found out that groups in the forces had to be stopped from operating the Ouija board.

"The Ouija board is a means of communicating with the collective subconscious of the group operating it. So you've got to recognize that group nature. For instance, if a Ouija message suggests that you change your job, you can sit and say to yourself, "Well, I really am feeling that I want to change my job," and if you do that in a critical way, that's fine. But if you take it literally and go and change your job without really thinking it all out consciously, then you can really get in trouble.

"If there are several people around the board, there's a degree of telepathy going around, and you may be picking up someone else's deep-seated anxieties and, so to speak, "owning them" yourself when really they're not yours at all! In other words, it might well be someone else in the group who is disturbed about their job and wanting a change, not you. In the Philip group we came to realize that when we got a particularly good specific response it was when there was a clear flash of telepathy going around the room. We were picking up each other's concerns and anxieties. You mustn't feel that they necessarily apply to you.

"We all have repressed anxieties. And repressed fears and repressed feelings and all sorts of repressed things in our lives! This is normal. Natural. It depends, in part, on how intense the people around the board are. The messages may be twisted and spurious, and they may be somebody else's subconscious mind just making up a nice little story for you.

"Let me give you an example of that. Someone here in Toronto was playing with the Ouija board and got very specific information about a schoolteacher being drowned in Lake Ontario. A date was given, an exact date, and the message from the board asked the board operators to contact the drowning victim's surviving brother—gave the brother's street address and all sorts of things, and the whole of that information was utterly false. The address didn't exist. The brother didn't exist. And nobody was known to have drowned in Lake Ontario on that date. And yet you can ask, "Who would invent something as absolutely specific as this?" That's what I mean about the subconscious mind being playful.

"People without background, without this kind of knowledge, can be very, very upset with what happens with a Ouija board. For a mature person interested in human psychology, it is fascinating to see how it works. If you can recognize the Ouija board for what it is—a way to communicate with your subconscious mind—it can help you, if you think about it, to analyze, criticize, deal with your own anxieties. Then it's *you* making the decision. But you really do have to set limits."

"Do some people come to the Toronto Society for Psychical Research because they're upset with their Ouija experiences?"

"We've had a lot of people come to us! Very upset, very disturbed. Usually we find that we can help them by sitting down and having a good, sensible talk. We compare their Ouija experience with the Philip experiment; and when we talk about it, then they understand. They're reassured and go away and don't play with the Ouija board anymore, which is good. . . . But let me tell you, the Ouija board is not a toy! For the lay person, the general public, it can be a very dangerous thing. It shouldn't be "played" with by anybody who is especially impressionable, not even impressionable adults, certainly not children.

"Thank you, Iris."

12

OUIJA
AND THE PRIEST
PARAPSYCHOLOGIST

Alphonsus Trabold is a rare combination of Franciscan priest, parapsychologist and historian of the occult. Talking with him, one senses a tremendous compassion and an easy strength. It is then that one recalls others saying of him that he is "an especially pious man." No doubt. But he is also a man with a solid sense of humor, quick to laugh, gentle, but intellectually tough-minded.

Father Trabold teaches a course titled "Psychical Research and the Nature of Man" in the theology department at St. Bonaventure University, St. Bonaventure, New York. He has assembled a personal library of more than two thousand volumes on the occult and the parapsychological. His résumé includes investigations with other priests, parapsychologists, demonologists, psychics and additional field research conducted under the auspices of the Psychical Research Foundation, Chapel Hill, North Carolina, for which Father Trabold is an official field reporter. He is also an active member of the (English) Society for Psychical Research, the American Society for Psychical Research and the Academy of Religion and Psychical Research.

On the Nature of the Ouija Board

FR. ALPHONSUS: The majority of parapsychologists, myself amongst them, would agree that the Ouija board is a form of automatism. An automatism is any unconscious movement used to express something in the unconscious mind. In other words, we pick up vast amounts of information and store it in the subconscious; that information then has the task of coming through to our conscious mind. Sometimes it comes through in dreams, sometimes it comes in the form of unconscious automatic movements, such as the Ouija board or automatic writing.

"The subconscious gets its information from many sources. Some information has been picked up subliminally; some of it may be picked up paranormally—for example, precognition, retrocognition, through clairvoyance or telepathy. Most of the information, probably, has been picked up through normal channels and simply forgotten.

"Any and all the information stored in the subconscious can be expressed through the Ouija board. Usually, expressions of lengthy material will end up as automatic writing."

"Don't Ouija board experimenters also function as spirit mediums?"

"A spirit medium is a go-between or link between the dead and the living. If a person uses the Ouija board as a means of communicating with the dead, then indeed such a person is acting as a spirit medium. However, if a person is using it as a means of simply releasing information from his subconscious mind, as I've explained, then he should not be called a spirit medium. A better word for him might be a 'psychic' or 'psychic sensitive.' "

"You've worked on possible possession and haunting cases with Ed and Lorraine Warren. Have you reached the same conclusions they reached, Father Trabold?"

"While we usually agree that certain paranormal phenomena do exist in these cases, we often differ as to the cause. The Warrens tend to see spirit influence more often than I do. Of the many cases I have dealt with over the years, I have *never* recommended a solemn exorcism. Many of these cases have been referred to me by other professionals—psychologists, psychiatrists, clergymen of all faiths, including some bishops."

"Have you never seen a possession case?"

"I don't believe so. Most of the classic symptoms or phenomena associated with spirit or demonic possession can be explained in terms of states other than possession. It's a very difficult judgment to make. That is why the Church demands great caution and seeks the aid of other sciences, especially psychology and parapsychology."

"But the Warrens seem so sure they're dealing with cases of demonic possession all the time."

"The Warrens are a very dedicated couple who have investigated many cases over the years. The certitude of their conclusions may result from their very close involvement in many difficult cases. While I truly respect their sincerity and extensive experience, in fairness I must state that I do not always agree with their convictions. Other parapsychologists have expressed this view also. In this field, there is surely room for different approaches and different opinions."

"The Warrens are very fearful of the Ouija board. They suggested that I bury mine under eighteen inches of dirt and sprinkle the site with holy water."

"I disagree with that entirely. A Catholic is forbidden to use the Ouija board as a means of communicating with the dead or with evil spirits. However, he is not forbidden to use it as an automatism, that is, as a means of expressing knowledge hidden in the subconscious mind."

"Then what are the actual dangers of Ouija usage, if any?"

"The great danger, I believe, is not from spirit entities, although there may be a few cases where they could be involved. But using any kind of automatism—including the Ouija board, definitely—to open the door to the subconscious can be dangerous. It brings in a food of information that the conscious mind might simply not be ready to handle. Another danger would be becoming obsessed with its use. Even such worthwhile practices as meditation may cause difficulties. Once we unlock the unconscious mind, we must be prepared to meet whatever is revealed; some persons are not prepared.

"Such excellent groups as the charismatics and Pentacostals have certain practices that may allow the subconscious to burst forth in their members. If this continues to happen to a person when he or she is alone, without the support and guidance of the group, he or she may then suffer some very bad effects. For example, the person may become confused and disoriented; in extreme cases the person may hallucinate."

"Is this the reason for saying that it is not a good idea to work with the Ouija board while alone?"

"I'd say so. That's a good rule of thumb."

"But it is okay, under some circumstances, to work with the Ouija board?"

"Yes, if used for a proper purpose. I believe that if valid messages are communicated through the Ouija board, they are usually psychic in nature, as I explained, and not the work of spirits. But, of course, I do have to leave the door open a crack. If people survive death, as we believe they do, and if there is such a thing as a demon, there is a possibility that such spirits, human or demonic, could interfere."

"And you have known of cases in which people suffered difficulties because they worked with the Ouija board?"

"I do know of people who have *abused* the Ouija board and have had disturbances break out in their homes, mostly because the use of the board caused their own psychic powers to break forth. I know of cases in which kids who had worked with the Ouija board were later struck by the planchette when no one was near it; it just suddenly sailed off the board by itself and struck one of the kids. That's an example of PK, psychokinesis. I had another case, a young girl, who became obsessed with automatic writing. Her life and her family's life almost became submerged in it. It really harmed them."

"What's the basic curative response to that sort of thing?"

"Just don't do it anymore. Don't use the Ouija board. Don't do automatic writing."

"When someone comes to you with serious Ouija-induced problems, how do you deal with them: as a priest or as a parapsychologist?"

"Usually as a combination of both. My goal as a priest is to help them the best way I can, so I call on all my knowledge, that is, of mysticism, spirituality, pastoral experience and parapsychology. But I've found that most cases I've dealt with can be explained in terms of the psychic rather than the supernatural. I've never come across a case where I could really say, without any doubts whatsoever, 'This is a spirit!' "

"What about hauntings? Is that spirit manifestation?"

"It could be. The difficulty is that there probably are many kinds of hauntings, each with its own special explanation. For example, it may be a case of merely misinterpreting some natural phenomenon, such as light or sound. Or it may be a case of fraud; some people lie to get attention. Even when real paranormal phenomena do take place, we can't always be sure if this is due to the presence of a spirit. In poltergeist cases, for example, it is commonly believed that a living human subject, often at the age of puberty, is causing the physical disturbances through his or her power of PK (psychokinesis). Ghosts (apparitions) have a number of explanations. Some believe these are due to a kind of psychic residue or imprint left behind by a person who has died. Some believe we all may have a kind of psychic double or energy body which we leave behind when we die and which may retain many of our characteristics and activities. It could remain behind in a certain place while its spirit passed on to another life. Sometimes such entities may borrow psychic energy from people now living in that place. For example, three or four families may live in a particular house and never experience any kind of manifestation. Then a certain person or family comes in, and the phenomena commence. It could be that the newcomers contribute psychic energy, acting as a kind of psychic battery."

"When investigating phenomena of this haunting sort, what is it you look for?"

"I try to eliminate the explanations already discussed: fraud, illusion, hallucination, et cetera. If I can do this, then I look for some paranormal cause such as the psychic theories given: a PK subject, a psychic residue or psychic double. If these explanations seem to be inadequate, then and only then do I look for a supernatural cause, that is, the presence of some dead person or a demon. To establish this presence, I look in particular for some kind of intelligent communication, some very definite purpose. From the point of view of theology, we believe that God is in control and that once you die you are judged, and you are given a particular state to go into."

"Such as?"

"For example, what we used to call purgatory. It is possible, of course, that a person could be assigned to a temporary state in order that he or she may be more perfected or made ready for the final union with God. And in that state the person would know why he was there. For example, I think it's possible that a person could be earth-bound, but God would tell him or her that; and the person certainly wouldn't be there just to scare people. He would know that he is dead and why he is now in a particular state."

"Do the earthbound communicate with the earth living?"

"I believe God could allow loved ones to come back sometime to help their loved ones on earth. That's possible. But I don't believe we can summon spirits, what we would call evocative spiritualism. I don't believe that."

"But the earthbound do communicate?"

"With God's permission, I believe, some kind of spirit could come across. But the initiative would come from their side. Here's where we differ from spiritualism. Their idea is that we can initiate contact on this side. I don't believe we can. I believe there is a gap between the living and the dead, and only with God's permission for a good holy purpose would He allow someone to come across. This would include not only persons in purgatory, but also those in heaven. Even demons require God's permission to manifest on earth.

"I believe that the bond of love between humans is so strong it cannot be broken by death. We're concerned with the dead, you know, and hope they're happy; and they're concerned with us, and they're in a position to help us because they're already on the other side. I'm very sure they're aware of what we're doing; and when they can, with God's permission, they help us, mostly in ways we're not aware of. But now and then I think they could in a paranormal way break through and help us in that way, too."

On Reincarnation

"Some of today's Christians are trying to accommodate the idea of reincarnation with Christianity, but as a theologian, I cannot accept it. First of all there's the Bible; second, there's Catholic tradition, neither of which seems to support this theory. I understand that Christ alone saves us. But in reincarnation, you're more or less saving yourself. In my mind that attitude simply blocks out the great work that Christ has done; the notion that salvation is ultimately His work. When I'm lecturing and people ask me what my attitude toward reincarnation is, I usually give them two answers, one as a theologian, the other from the point of view of parapsychology. Parapsychology seems to give us some evidence for reincarnation. Ian Stevenson's work has demonstrated past knowledge in very young children, for example. But as I explained before, there are strong theological reasons for my not accepting reincarnation as a reality at this time. But, you know, my mind is open."

"Aren't there alternate theories?"

"I think so. And if you can find one or more alternatives to explain the facts documented by Dr. Stevenson and others, then you can't finally insist on interpreting them in terms of reincarnation. It might be a temporary spirit influence. A dead person could be influencing some living person and telling that living person things about the dead person's former life."

"Wouldn't that be a temporary possession?"

"Yes. An alternate theory allows for some kind of univeral psychic memory, the idea that all our thoughts and actions are recorded in that memory. Jung's collective unconsciousness is one way of expressing this. So it could be that some people tune into that memory and are getting the information that way. But I believe the human person is too unique and precious to be jumping around into a variety of different lives. Traditional Christianity says a person is given one chance to choose God or not, and that he or she is given sufficient knowledge and grace to make the right choice."

"Thank you, Father Trabold."

13

AUTOMATISMS AS THE INDUCERS OF PSYCHOSES AND AS A CURE

"The unwitting use of automatisms like the Ouija board can induce psychosis."

This is from a letter written to me by the foremost expert on this subject in all Europe, Dr. Hans Bender.

Dr. Bender's credentials as a scientist are of the highest order. He obtained his Ph.D. from Bonn University in 1936 upon the presentation of his thesis, "Psychic Automatisms." He obtained his M.D. from Strasbourg University in 1942 and held academic posts in psychology and clinical psychology at the Universities of Bonn and Strasbourg. In 1950, Dr. Bender founded the Institute for Border Areas of Psychology and Mental Hygiene in Freiburg, West Germany, and is the Institute's present director. He is also professor emeritus of the department of psychology and border areas of psychology at Freiburg University.

Dr. Bender is the author of "Mediumistic Psychoses," a breakthrough study that clearly establishes the dangers of automatisms like the Ouija board. This study was published in German in the *Journal of Parapsychology and Border Areas of Psychology* (*Zeitschrift für Parapsychologie und Grenzgebiete der Psychologie,* Vol. 2, 1959, pp. 173–201), and in the book *Telepathy, Clairvoyance and Psychokinesis* (*Telepathie, Hellsehen und Psychokinese*), 1983, Piper Publications, Munich.

The discussion that follows is based on "Mediumistic Psychoses" as translated (for this book) by Carl Rothfuss, instructor of foreign languages at Central Michigan University.

Dr. Bender's 1936 doctoral thesis was in part an overview of the psychology of the subconscious and non-sensate perception, a testing of several automatisms in the laboratory, an inquiry into case histories of mediumistic psychoses and the mechanics of these psychoses.

Although the Ouija board is not specifically mentioned in the doctoral thesis, it must be pointed out that Dr. Bender includes the Ouija board in the category of automatisms. What is said of other automatisms is also true of the Ouija board.

Mediumistic Psychoses and Automatism

Dr. Bender, in the course of his studies, came across people who were suffering from some sort of mental illness; for the most part, these people were identified as suffering from schizophrenia, yet they exhibited certain symptoms that were at odds with the classic definition of schizophrenia. Dr. Bender found a common link in these people: at one time or another they had all practiced some form of automatism.

He distinguished two forms or kinds of automatisms: the motor form, an expression of the subconscious processes through involuntary muscular control; and the sensorial form, which has to do with involuntary experiences associated with the senses—seeing, hearing, touching, etc. Sensorial experiences are rare, and require some kind of predisposition. Ouija involves the involuntary muscular control . . . and is common.

Dr. Bender gave numerous case histories. He reported a woman who did automatic writing in the script of her deceased husband. She was right-handed, but the spirit writing was produced by her left hand. The familiar handwriting revealed to her many things she didn't know before. After three intensive weeks of automatic writing, the woman began hearing voices. The voices, initially friendly, soon began demanding negative, compulsive actions on her part. This acute stage lasted for four weeks. This was followed by a residual condition: a chorus of unwanted spirit voices threatened her while making impossible demands. The woman did not respond to suggestive therapy.

A second victim began work with a spiritualist circle. While glass-rapping, she suddenly heard a voice she didn't recognize. As she continued with this form of automatism, she began to hear knocking on walls and in corners. Soon, disembodied voices began speaking to her in an uninterrupted flow. The voice blasphemed her, prophesying disaster for her and issuing destructive commands. She was able to seek professional help only by exerting her will with all her strength. After six weeks of suggestive therapy, she was released from a clinic as cured.

One victim, who practiced table-rapping, once saw a disembodied hand pointing to a river. She jumped in, but was rescued against her will.

Another case involved 39-year-old twin sisters who became involved with table-rapping and automatic writing after reading the novel *The Sin Against the Spirit,* which encourages the use of automatisms without thoroughly discussing them. One of the twins began receiving dictated messages from her deceased father. She soon began hearing disembodied voices. At her "father's" suggestion, she slit open her wrists. At the time, she was an inpatient at a clinic, having been diagnosed as schizophrenic. Her sister, too, attempted suicide, and was admitted to a clinic. Both received shock therapy and were eventually cured.

Dr. Bender asserted that the diagnosis of schizophrenia was based merely on the idea that, since they were twins, they probably shared a predisposition to schizophrenia. But Dr. Bender holds that their being twins is not essentially relevant to their illnesses. What is important was that both women were intimate friends who, together and separately, compulsively practiced automatic writing and table-rapping.

Yet another case Dr. Bender discussed in his paper involved a 69-year-old widow and retired librarian, Regina S. She began running a pendulum over an alphabet display. When this form of Ouija became compulsive, voices began tormenting her. Soon the torment became physical. While ordered to imagine perverse erotic scenes, she was made to sit perfectly still for hours at a time. She was commanded to hold her hands in ice water until the pain became unbearable. This torture went on until the victim tore herself away from the voices and sought treatment. She was treated and successfully cured in a short time.

Dr. Bender contends that there are real differences between schizophrenic and mediumistic psychoses. The pathogenesis, or source, and the process of the two illnesses are quite different. In both there are clearly structured syndromes usually thought of as the essence of "being schizophrenic." The features of the syndrome include thoughts heard aloud, a slipping away of thoughts, mind reading, voices accompanying actions, hallucinations, inner dialogues, and delusions of influence and control.

But the premorbid personalities of the schizophrenic and the psychically gifted differ radically. The premorbid schizophrenic is autistic, anxious, barely suggestible and hardly imitative. The premorbid psychically gifted personality, on the other hand, is lively, social (often in excess), emotionally likable, fluctuating in personality values and strongly suggestive. Unlike the schizophrenic, the psychically gifted have a great tendency to imitate, often to the point of unconscious identification. This tendency to unconscious identification is in itself a sign of vulnerability or softness in the personality structure.

In addition, schizophrenic psychosis seems to lead to a massive destruction of the self which is thought to be inevitable and irreversible. Mediumistic psychosis, in comparison, is reversible. "Whereas the schizophrenic self-disturbance . . . appears as the symptom of a fundamental disturbance attacking the core of the personality in a presumably unavoidable fashion," Dr. Bender wrote, "the psychogenic ('hysterical') self-disturbance can be viewed as an *understandable, avoidable, reversible* functional disintegration of the personality." [Stress added.]

Mediumistic psychosis is a disintegration that does "not shatter the psyche into pieces; rather it creates functional units which act more or less independently of each other. It is not a splitting-off, but a functional liberation of partial systems which justify the image of geared events in a multidimensional organism rather than a fission."

Dr. Bender pointed out that, predisposition or not, these artificial personality splits are caused by exposure to automatisms and the use of them. In other words, these psychic instruments play a functional role in the development of the psychosis. Mediumistic psychosis is a particular kind of illness that cannot be entirely explained away in terms of predispositions and personal circumstances. The psychosis could have been prevented if the automatism had been avoided. Also, if the mechanism of the automatism is understood for what it is—communication with the operator's "Other"—some of these problems could also be avoided. When the person confuses the results of the automatism with spiritualism, his psyche is more vulnerable to severe shock.

The shock comes when the messages received are felt to be "alien to the self and inaccessible to voluntary control." There is a tendency on the part of the subconscious to personify itself. This personification is reinforced because the subconscious mind consists of "autonomous psychic realms" and has at its disposal the entire memory bank of the total personality—much more information than is ordinarily available to the conscious ego. The conscious self cannot recall the psychic events embedded in the subconscious. When bits of this material are suddenly presented in a personified way, the experience can be overwhelming.

Dr. Bender concluded that although mediumistic psychoses have symptoms in common with hysterical self-disturbances, these psychoses are to be distinguished from schizophrenic states, rather than understood as a mere subcategory with occult tinges. Mediumistic psychosis is a transitory psychic disturbance caused by the uncritical use of "spiritualist practices and set in motion by the affective shock of misunderstood other-world practices."

This distinction is vitally important in diagnosis. Mediumistic psychosis can be cured, *if properly identified,* in a jshort time. Regina S. was rapidly cured because Dr. Bender correctly identified her problem and she was willing to rationally analyze what had been happening to her.

It is sad to think how many victims of mediumistic psychoses have spent long periods of unnecessary time in asylums because they were incorrectly diagnosed as schizophrenic.

Ouija Therapeutics

Though the obsessive use of automatisms can cause psychosis, automatisms can be used as a tool by professionals to cure psychosis. Anita M. Muhl, M.D., research psychiatrist, served as assistant physician at St. Elizabeth's Hospital in Washington, D.C., and as chief of the division of special education for the California State Department of Education until 1929. Dr. Muhl made extremely successful use of automatic writing to delve into the repressions of her patients—many of whom were considered functionally incurable—to unearth memories and idea associations. Her classic yet largely ignored book, *Automatic Writing: An Approach to the Unconscious,* was first published in 1930 in Leipzig, Germany, and reprinted in English by Helix Press in 1963. According to Barbara Honegger, *Automatic Writing* is "still the best available statement of a psychological theory of automatic writing."

To achieve release from repression or other pathological mental illnesses, it is necessary that repressed material be brought up from the subconscious to the conscious. In therapy, this is traditionally done using a variety of tools or techniques in combination. These include word and idea association, memory recall development and dream analysis.

As a therapeutic tool, dream analysis is so effective it is often referred to as the "royal road to the unconscious." But dream analysis is difficult—time-consuming and costly. It often requires years of patient training and the outlay of large amounts of money.

According to Dr. Muhl, automatic writing is a far more effective tool than dream analysis, and it achieves the same results. Used in conjunction with other therapeutic tools, automatic writing can achieve "miraculous" cures in surprisingly short periods of time, often in as few as six or eight sessions; and of course, at much less dollar cost.

The material revealed by automatic writing can be dangerous. But in a therapeutic setting, the therapist can withhold upsetting material even while taking curative advantage of the messages revealed. The patient need not be exposed directly to the contents of the automatic writing.

Dr. Muhl discovered numerous therapeutic uses of automatic writing. They include the releasing of conflicts, the obtaining of material for use in sublimation, the recall of forgotten incidents not associated with conflicts and the releasing of energy "for use in actual adjustment."

Who can benefit from this treatment? The fact is, almost everyone can automatic write: the sane, the neurotic, the psychotic. And those who can't automatic write can probably automatic spell with a Ouija board.

Some of Dr. Muhl's patients did more than write automatically. They also drew pictures and portraits automatically. The symbolic contents of these drawings were then revealed through the use of later automatic writing.

Automatic writing also occurred in various rare forms. Some people were able to write automatically with both hands simultaneously, each hand producing different scripts and messages. Some messages were inverted or written in reverse mirror script. (This mirror writing is technically named "strephographia.") Some dual-personality patients hallucinated while automatic writing; the hallucinations in these cases often described the typically briefer automatic writing messages in greater detail; this was a great boon to the therapist. Many wrote using a penmanship totally different from their ordinary penmanship. Some wrote automatically in the hand of friends or relatives, sometimes in the hands of the deceased.

Dr. Muhl rarely had trouble getting her patients to write automatically. The patients needed to be relaxed before they began, so she typically distracted their conscious attention by simple means (requesting mathematical or word puzzle solving, for example), and the automatic writing usually flowed revealingly. She also promoted ease of writing by using a simple homemade sling that allowed her patients to hold their writing arms and hands slightly above the surface of the paper. Occasionally she would hypnotize patients before they wrote, or she would leave them with a post-hypnotic suggestion.

The Psycho-Spiritual Dangers of Automatic Writing

Although automatic writing may be an invaluable means of plumbing the subconscious, it can be very dangerous as well. Much of the material revealed by automatic writing is destructive. It refers particularly to the pathological state, so when repressed material is released in this direct, unedited way, the automatic writer could be incapable of dealing positively and creatively with the messages that come through.

Unsupervised, uninformed, compulsive automatic writing done by a severely or even mildly repressed person is destructive. As Dr. Muhl explained it, "These particular experiments in multiple involuntary expressions are dangerous for the amateur and should be avoided. The possibility of complete fragmentation of the personality is too great."

To prevent difficulties and possible tragedies, Dr. Muhl formulated a series of Rules for Safety. They are:

1. Always write at the same time every day and for short periods only (not over fifteen or twenty minutes to begin with).
2. Learn to work under distraction—i.e., reading. This will preclude any possibility of so-called trance condition developing (unintentionally).
3. Learn to evaluate by means of free association (especially) all material produced. This will help not only in interpretation of the writing but will help also to bring to light hidden unconscious motives.
4. Make use of all energy freed this way by directing it into constructive channels.

14

OUIJA AND THE HONEGGER THEORY

ormerly Office of Policy Development, White House, policy analyst, and more recently with the U.S. Department of Justice, Barbara Honegger is the first person in the United States to be graduated with an advanced degree in experimental parapsychology (John F. Kennedy University, Orinda, California, 1981). She is a past president of the Parapsychology Research Group, an associate member of the Parapsychological Association, was a research associate in theoretical parapsychology at Washington Research Center, San Francisco, and twice a research assistant at the Hoover Institution at Stanford University, earning two medals of distinguished service. In addition to being an invited speaker at the Smithsonian Institution in 1981 and 1982 (topic: Psi and the Brain), she is also the author of numerous articles on psi published in both professional and popular journals. (Psi, the first letter of the Greek word *psyche,* designates all forms of ESP and psychokinetic phenomena.)

I spoke with her about the Ouija board and her new, revealing theories of mediumship.

"The Ouija board is a tool. Like any other tool, it can be used for good or bad, but in and of itself, like psi, it is neutral. I'd like to emphasize that Ouija is just one case in a broad range of phenomena.

"Mediumship is much more common and diverse than people think. It extends to automatic writing, bibliomancy, divination and direct-voice phenomena, as well as the Ouija board. All of these forms are communication by words or symbols, the same way we communicate our mental thoughts in our normal everyday consciousness. This is no coincidence, yet very few people have picked up on this similarity so far.

"I contend, and there's strong evidence to support my argument, that *each* brain hemisphere has a separate and conscious ego. There are at least two personalities cohabiting in every *normal* human. Each hemisphere of the brain has a self-reflective consciousness and a substratum that allows us to sign and symbolize. I'm talking about a supersense, an inter-modality sense. That means whatever we feel, see, hear, smell, taste or touch gets channeled into a supersense that abstracts these sensations and allows for language, conceptualization and abstraction.

"My main point is that there are *two* such centers, one for each hemisphere, and they are totally separate. Furthermore, when one of the two centers is active, a neurophysiological mechanism actively inhibits the other from expressing its mental contents.

"This means the 'unconscious' is always thinking and aware. It's self-reflective and it needs to express itself from time to time. For instance, when the ego consciousness is missing important information, one's normal inhibition is overridden so that the other side can communicate its knowledge."

"Let me get this straight. The unconscious is really a second conscious ego that wants to communicate but normally can't when the ego consciousness—the 'I'—is in control of the physical body. But when it is important enough, the conscious 'unconscious' gets its message through?"

"Yes. And there's a physical parallel to this. The corpus callosum is the part of the brain that connects the two hemispheres. Still—somehow—when the corpus callosum is cut, communication between the two hemispheres continues (although not on the same level of efficiency). We may not understand yet how the egos in each hemisphere communicate with each other, but when they do, we know that as spiritualization. And when you finally understand that your overriding consciousness is not alone in your mind, the process of spiritualization accelerates.

"For this to happen, the Normal Everyday Awake ego must first acknowledge the existence of the other, and vice versa. What happens then is a period of mutual discovery, crises, et cetera, just as in a marriage. A lot depends on the two personalities."

"So there's also a personality associated with each awareness?"

"Yes. As I'm talking with you now, my left-hemisphere entity is talking with *your* left-hemisphere entity. But within each individual there is also a right-hemisphere entity, and inter-hemispheric communication is possible. The more this communication takes place, the more spiritualized the 'I'— the left entity—becomes. Furthermore, our right-hemisphere entity can communicate with other right-hemisphere entities. That, in my opinion, is what we call telepathic communication: right-to-right communication, *across* brains. My left-hemisphere ego cannot communicate to your left-hemisphere ego except through 'normal' voluntary motor means, using the muscles of speech.

"Each individual right-hemisphere-associated consciousness has its own strategy or style of finally getting through to the left consciousness. Some people play around with the Ouija board and discover it that way. Some people through bibliomancy. Some through automatic writing. Some through dreams. What's important is that the communication is made and that the Other is recognized as *normal*. Both have an unconscious in Freud's sense—the unconscious being the contents of the long-term memory to which each ego consciousness had or has access.

"Freud had a hierarchical view, but just *one* hierarchy. What I'm proposing is that there are *two* hierarchies: two long-term memories *and* two short-term memories, two 'working memories' for each hemisphere—and an unconscious memory for each, which may overlap. This is developed in my paper, 'A Neuropsychological Theory of Automatic Behavior' in the July–August 1980 edition of *Parapsychology Review.*"

Ouija, Mediumship and 'The Other'

"The Ouija board is one form of automatic writing, which is one form of mediumship. And mediumship is an expression, in one form, of the alterego, the Other entity. The Ouija puck, the pendulum, the dowsing rod—they all do the same thing; they're simply amplifiers. They amplify very small motor signals. And very small signals are usually as much as your Other side can organize.

"Your overriding consciousness can thwart the Other's expressions, even on the muscular level. But the *involuntary* motor system is not inhibited. So you have to have a way of amplifying the Other's instructions to the *non*-inhibited musculature. And that's exactly what the Ouija board puck and other amplifiers do."

Ouija and the Earthbound

"When Matthew Manning was a schoolboy (now he's in his twenties), he was the center of the most phenomenal, repeatable poltergeist activity recorded in modern history. The poltergeist phenomena followed him, so he was obviously in focus. One day, while a poltergeist was in progress, he had an urge to pick up a pen. The pen, as it were, moved by itself. When Matthew allowed himself to write automatically, the poltergeist stopped. The point is that poltergeist activity is an unfocused form of mediumship. Now, in all this kind of activity, the idea is to home in on the entity's preferred mode of communication; and that is exactly what Matthew did. He learned that as long as he spent a certain amount of time automatic writing, the poltergeist would cease. Later, he responded to yet another urge to pick up a brush, and he became an exceptional automatic painter. In his book, *The Link*, there are reproductions of these automatic paintings."

"About a third of the people who responded to my national Ouija survey say that they communicate with earthbounds."

"The priority communicators are usually thought of as past entities who have problems. If they didn't have problems, they wouldn't still be around. They'd be evolving. It is wise to set aside a set, limited period of time to help these earthbounds and never exceed it.

"In the Matthew Manning case, these lingering spirits desperately needed someone to release them. One can think of that as doing a great service. According to this point of view, if you want to work with a Ouija board or some other form of mediumship, you should do so with a healing motive, not simply curiosity. You should ask yourself, 'How can I help in such a way that the entities that need help will respect my sovereignty and I theirs?' That's the understanding that's needed. You have to see these earthbound entities for what they are, entities that have problems, entities that have to be released."

"And how does one release them?"

"Essentially, they are released when they know that someone else knows their history. 'The truth is known, now I can go on.' It's the knowing, in and of itself, the acknowledgment of the data by another, that liberates. The medium, the person who finds the data out and acknowledges it, doesn't have to do anything more; doesn't have to go to court, to the press, or write a book. The sheer experience of verification is what releases.

"Anyone who doesn't feel he or she is 'together' enough as an adult should not work with the Ouija board or any kind of mediumship. If you can't counsel another embodied human being, you can't help the earthbound either."

"Should one interact with the entities as if they were embodied?"

"Yes, and be kind and healing. Release them by accepting their message for what it is. Think about the times of trouble in your own life. You confided in a friend; and when you walked away from that conversation, you felt much relieved, just knowing that you didn't have to bear your experience alone. And your friend felt relieved too, having helped you.

"Remember, spirits are earthbound for a reason, usually when death has occurred suddenly. Generally, the dying person knows he or she is going to die about three days before death occurs, at least unconsciously. That knowledge gives the person three days to prepare, to take care of business, to forgive themselves and others. If the earthbound was deprived of the severing process, it still has some unfinished business to take care of. All that the spirit needs is an instrument to be its body for the short time it takes to communicate its final needs."

"Isn't that a possession?"

"It might seem that way. Most so-called possessions are of very short duration. In many cultures, fasts that last for an entire month are conducted. This allows earthbounds to come through and work their problems out, finish up their unfinished business."

"Some view communication with the dead as sinful or devilish."

"There's nothing evil or devilish about communicating

with those you believe are dead. There's no fundamental difference, in my opinion, between talking on the telephone with someone you've never met and using the Ouija board. Both are 'disembodied' communication.''

Summary Ouija Precautions

"The seeker has total control over what to ask and whom to ask. The seeker has total freedom. Still the Ouija board can be dangerous, but not because it is evil. It's dangerous in the sense that it is powerful; in the sense that healing energy is powerful. It must be used with caution, and then it can do great good.

"I wouldn't recommend its use to any adult who doesn't know who he or she is . . . or to *any* child. This is very, very important. You need a very strong sense of who you are and of what your mental contents and message patterns are. That way you will recognize what is not yours. It's a question of being able to recognize the message. Unless the medium recognizes a message as coming from another, there is no release. If there is release, then it's powerful and positive.

"To be comfortable and therefore safe with any form of mediumship, you need to be able to recognize the YOU and the NOT-YOU, and know that both are all right.''

"Thank you, Barbara.''

OUIJA

AND THE PRACTICAL PERSON

15

BEFORE YOU OUIJA

Most people interviewed for this book suggest that
the only sure way to avoid trouble with the Ouija
board is simply to avoid working with it. And
because the dangers of the Ouija seem to be real, anyone
intent on experimenting with it should take certain pre-
session precautions. There are certain people, however,
who should never use the board or experiment with any
Ouija-like device, no matter how tempting or what the
circumstances.

Who Should Never Use the Board

Even those people who swear by the board warn that Ouija
is not a pastime for minors: not youngsters, not teenagers.

No one—regardless of age—should experiment with
the Ouija if they are using mind-altering drugs, legal or
illegal. This includes alcohol and marijuana just as much as
cocaine, LSD and heroin. Drugs are catalysts for negative
experiences.

Anyone who has any type of emotional or physical
disorder should avoid using the board. Successful Ouija
experimentation necessarily draws a considerable amount of
energy from the operator. This is serious in several ways.
First, it depletes a body already struggling for the reestab-

lishment of healthy inner balances. Second, illness or disease is in and of itself a negative state. Working the board will mirror physical negativity, perhaps intensify it and yield undesirable results. Third, a state of poor health often increases suggestibility. This lowering of the operator's ability to analyze and criticize emerging Ouija messages must be clearly understood as disadvantageous.

Also, all Fundamentalist Christians or people who believe in the existence of Satan and the demonic essence of the Ouija board should obviously not use the instrument. These beliefs almost guarantee a negative Ouija experience. Despite conscious intentions, the literalist religionist brings a subconscious self-condemnation to working the board.

What You Should Know Before You Begin
Limit Your Experiences

The first rule of thumb is to limit your Ouija experiments. Paul Beard, the noted psychic researcher, thinks that obsession is the single greatest danger of Ouija experimentation. "The first line of defense is for the host [operator] to adhere strictly to the rule not to consent to write [Ouija] for more than one hour a week," he warns. "If the influence suggests or requests more of the sensitive host upon whatever pretext, this should be considered as the strongest possible warning signal."

Be Positive

Like attracts like, whether positive or negative. So it is vital that the Ouija board operator approach the experiment in a positive manner. Avoid working the Ouija when feeling angry, revengeful, confused or depressed. The Law of Attraction or karma will return these emotions to the unwitting operator. If you feel any negativity whatsoever, put off Ouija experimentation until emotional equilibrium has returned and forgiveness and love are once again dominant.

Petty, self-serving motives generate petty, self-serving Ouija responses. In this regard, a vulgar curiosity should not be confused with a real and sincerely felt need to know. A good point to remember: if you should begin to feel a negative emotion while working with the Ouija, stop. If the Ouija itself should suggest that a session be concluded, stop. It doesn't pay to push on. There's always a later time if it's allowed to develop.

Work with a Partner

Always work with a partner—*never work alone*. Ouija experiences can be emotionally powerful, sometimes frightening, disturbing or overwhelming. Working with others helps assure a proper response if distress should occur.

Be sure to pick someone you like and respect and *trust*. The messages that surface in your experiment may embarrass you. They may give away secrets that you'd rather not go public with.

To get the best results, you and your partner must approach the experiment good-naturedly but seriously. Talk between yourselves before you approach the board. Feel very positive. Assume you will be successful. Expect the board to "talk" to you.

Never take Ouija messages for granted—whether they are addressed to you or your partner. Informed, honest criticism is important both while receiving messages and while considering the *content* of the messages.

No matter what you think about the Ouija board at the outset, at some point you will probably become a bit apprehensive—not quite sure where the message are really coming from. It will be almost impossible for you not to think about "voices from the other side," "spirits" and "supernatural entities." So, I suggest that no matter how straight your thinking is about the Ouija, you should take precautions against what you might later perceive to be demons or negative spirits that want to harm you.

Prayer Before and After Prayer

The saying of a prayer before and after each Ouija session is recommended by many serious Ouija operators. No particular prayer has evolved. It's the individual's choice. Many people use the Lord's Prayer (Our Father Who Art in Heaven . . .) In Chapter 7, the spirit Thomas recommended that once your hands are in place on the board, you say—aloud or mentally—"Oh God, Keeper of the Universe, I release my mind to the flow of the power of the universe. I desire only good that I may learn and develop. Protect me from any negative forces and surround me with pure love."

The visualization of a protective white light is considered by some to be a prayer. It's sometimes called the Christ light, but it need not be thought of in that particular theological way. (Some kabbalists have spoken of a "sapphire light" that surrounds the body.) The important thing is that the light visualization is a protective act that helps the Ouija operator focus consciousness in a creative, positive way. They recommend you pray in the way you feel comfortable and happy with; a standardized prayer or one of your own invention is fine. The important thing is that it be done sincerely.

Harold Sherman, president and executive director of the ESP Research Associates Foundation of Little Rock, Arkansas, first came to national attention as a psychic more than forty years ago. He conducted his first successful experiment with long-distance telepathy by communicating with the famous Arctic explorer, Sir Hubert Wilkins. The telepathic messages traveled from New York to the Arctic.

"I have a meditation that I developed years ago," says Sherman. "Since then it's been used by many thousands of people, people who have been disturbed or even possessed. It enables them to demagnetize themselves, to free themselves of low-grade spirit entities or the obsessions that at times overwhelm them. Thousands of people have gone to psychiatrists and spent a lot of money and time trying to get away from the influences they've become involved with. Then they've been freed with just this simple statement. It's been thoroughly tested. It should be repeated, preferably aloud, in privacy, before and after working with the Ouija board. Whenever the need is felt, this declaration reminds the speaker of the oneness with God."

> I am never alone.
> God the Father is always with me.
> My soul, my identity—that something which says, "I am I" to me—is an eternal gift from God, the Great Intelligence.
> I can never lose myself, because this self is a part of God.
> I am part of God, and God has a great purpose in life for me which He is revealing day by day as I grow in strength of body, mind and spirit.
> I am well and strong. I have the power to overcome all things within me.
> In God's care, no harm can befall me.
> I now give myself over to God's protection and I will follow His guidance day by day.

"How to Guard Against 'Possession' "

The above heading is in quotes because it is also the original title of an essay (*Spiritual Frontiers,* Autumn 1970) written by psychic researcher Paul Beard. Beard is the retired president of the College of Psychic Studies, London, England. The college is not, as its name suggests, a center for the scientific or parapsychological study of the paranormal. Rather, it is a well-known organization "devoted to finding in spiritualism further evidence for survival after death."

Beard's essay not only concerns how to guard yourself

from possession; it also tells how a person already ravaged by an obsessing entity can fight back. The fight, one hardly needs to say, is not easy.

First, all Ouija or other forms of psychic experimentation must stop. There can be no equivocating. If any object or activity has even a hint of the psychical or occult about it, it must be strictly avoided. This includes automatic writing, astrology, Tarot cards, dowsing, the use of the pendulum, even TM and other forms of meditation. The victim must not acknowledge the invading entity in any way. The Japanese have a phrase for it: "ignoring unto death." The obsession victim must concentrate on the practical affairs of ordinary daily life. "As long as the oppressor can talk or think with the victim, it will result in his strengthening its hold," Paul Beard insists.

There are other tasks to do: prime among them, the victim must identify and correct the weakness in character that allowed the observer to enter and take control. And as the Warrens (Chapter 8) recommended, the victim should pray and visualize himself completely encircled in a cloud of brilliantly bright white light.

In order to write this essay, Mr. Beard evidently spent many long, difficult hours of research and investigation. It is interesting to know that now Mr. Beard is quoted as strongly recommending that the Ouija board "not be researched or written about."

16

HOW TO GET THE BEST RESULTS FROM YOUR OUIJA EXPERIMENTS

You've read about the joy the Ouija board has brought to some people's lives; you've also read how Ouija has destroyed some people. There seem to be a lot more reasons *not* to experiment with the Ouija or any of the other Ouija-like phenomena than to experiment. However, some people find the idea irresistible and will want to try their hand at it as soon as they close this book. If that's the case; if you think such experimentation will enrich your life or help you learn more about yourself and the nature of reality, here are some tips to get the best results from your Ouija board.

To get started, you need a Ouija board and a pointer. You can buy one for about fifteen dollars, or you can make an alphabet board of your own in less than five minutes. It won't cost you anything and it will work as well as any. All you need for the board is a sheet of paper or cardboard or a piece of Masonite. Actually, any material with a smooth surface will do.

The store-bought board is Masonite approximately 18″ × 12″ inches. Yours should be at least that big, but it doesn't have to be rectangular. It can be round, diamond-shaped, triangular—whatever you like. You need a pencil, crayon or Magic Marker to print the letters of the alphabet and the numbers 0 to 9 on the board. That's all you really

A sample home-drawn Ouija board

need, but it would be helpful to add the words YES, NO, MAYBE, an ampersand (&) and a few punctuation marks. Since the pointer is going to slide across the board, its surface should be as smooth and slick as possible. If you're using wood or Masonite, you probably should wax the surface. If you're using a sheet of paper, you might put it under a plate of glass.

For a pointer you can use anything that will glide easily across the surface with little friction. A teacup turned upside down will work fine. So will a clear juice glass. Anything will work so long as it's big enough for you and your partner to rest the fingers of one hand on its top surface.

That's all the equipment you need to get started. To record the messages that you'll receive from the board, you'll need a pad of paper and a pencil or a tape recorder.

How to Work the Ouija Board

The mechanics of Ouija board experimentation—who sits where, how the fingers are placed on the planchette, the placement of the board, etc.—are not terribly important. People have individual reactions to the Ouija board, and what works for one person may not work for another. If you are sincerely interested in working the board, you will eventually discover what works best for you through trial and error.

Most people start off their Ouija experiment by sitting on chairs facing each other. They touch their knees together and balance the board on their knees. Each person rests one hand lightly on the board, and the fingers of the other hand very lightly on the planchette. (Too much pressure prevents the pointer from sliding smoothly.)

It is best that only one operator ask questions of the board. Questions may be agreed upon before the session begins. Initially, questions should be kept simple and direct. "Is anyone on the board?" "Will we communicate this evening?" "Are there any messages for us today?" Ask the questions patiently, efficiently. One way to test the results is to ask questions you know the answers to: "How old am I?" "How many letters are there in my middle name?"

If the question-and-answer method is not productive, abandon it. Simply rest your fingers lightly on the pointer and wait for the pointer to initiate communication. The board will volunteer statements if you give it the opportunity to do so. Once you have established communication, the conversation should flow easily.

With a beginner, the planchette may move reluctantly, and the first results may be incoherent or unreliable. People with strong psychic powers, however, have been known to cause the planchette to move even without touching it.

Beginners need to look at the letters on the board.

The planchette often moves wildly, overshooting a desired letter, then dashing back toward that letter. But this rarely happens to the experienced and developed operator. Some people can perform perfectly even though blindfolded or engaged in other activities such as talking or reading.

It has been said that when one of the operators takes his or her hand off the planchette, or when operators are changed, the planchette may move around madly until control is reestablished. Spiritualists view this as the spirits vying among themselves to communicate with the new operator. Some believers in the automatistic theory view this as pent-up psychic energy finding its release.

Record-keeping is an important aspect of Ouija communication. A diary or journal that includes all questions asked and all answers given is highly recommended. Date the entries. Messages can be written down when the planchette pauses or stops moving; or a third person can take dictation. Good record-keeping can be useful later for verifying messages, for planning further Ouija sessions and for continuity of conversation. Also, Ouija messages can be cryptic, and specific meanings won't become clear until some time has passed and the session records consulted.

Ouija messages are often given in a form of shorthand. For example, the letter "u" might be used to represent the word *you*. You may remember advertisements that read, "If u cn rd ths, u 2 cn lrn 2 tke shrthnd & ern bg $." Ouija messages can look something like that. Initials are frequently used instead of full names. After a regular communication is established, a personal shorthand usually develops.

Punctuation is another important part of good record-keeping. Most boards don't include punctuation marks, so it is up to the person writing down the dictation to do the punctuation, to determine where sentences begin and end, to establish paragraphing, etc. This is usually easy to do. But in cases where the messages seem cryptic, don't throw the message away. File it with the rest of the material, and you may later make sense of it in the light of further revelations.

Ouija messages can be given in languages other than your own. They can be slangy, or in dialect, or highly technical. They can be poetic or smutty.

Introductions are in order when you meet someone for the first time—even if it's through the Ouija board. Politely ask for personal details: name, age, where the individual is, what the individual wants. Ask if you can do something for the individual. Do they have a story they'd like to tell you? A message? Testimony?

Don't force the conversation. Don't make rude or selfish demands. Don't place the emphasis on yourself. And *do not take Ouija statements for granted.* Criticize! Analyze! Challenge! Express your doubts. Ask for proof.

If the planchette suddenly refuses to continue moving, don't insist that it do so. Don't push or force the issue. If you suddenly feel overwhelmed or threatened, stop immediately.

Final Words

If you choose to work the Ouija board after having read all this, I wish you good luck. May you find what you are looking for, and may it enrich your life.

If you have had any interesting Ouija experiences and are willing to share them, address your letter to:

OUIJA

Box 109
Barnes & Noble Books
Harper & Row, Publishers
10 East 53rd Street
New York, New York 10022

INDEX